STORE IT!

STORE IT!

WHERE TO PUT ALL THE THINGS YOU NEED TO KEEP

By Mervyn Kaufman
and the editors of
PointClickHome.com

POINTclick**HOME**

CONTENTS

INTRODUCTION

We acquire, we consume, we trash, and in addition we also store. Even items we haven't worn, used, or even looked at in years manage to get tucked away because we somehow feel we cannot function without them. The result is that our attics and basements, if we have either or both, and certainly our closets, are all packed to the walls and ceiling—often with items we should have disposed of long ago.

A lot of us complain repeatedly that our homes just aren't big enough to hold everything we need to keep there, although we probably know in our hearts that, even if we could double our living space overnight, we would gradually fill every nook and cranny and, once again, wonder aloud if there was any way to acquire more room.

Lack of space is certainly a challenge, but it is superseded in every instance by the answer to one succinct question: How best to use that space? Yes, we can buy and bring in more cabinets, cupboards, bookshelves, and chests. But before actually shopping, we must determine what we really don't need to keep anymore—and get rid of it. Then we should select the most likely and convenient places to store what we decide we have to keep.

In truth, there probably isn't a room in the house where we don't store something. Then, of course, there are outdoor spaces where storage capability is also essential. All such needs should be assessed; we shouldn't store anything we haven't examined and evaluated. Similarly, we shouldn't put away anything that we haven't labeled or identified clearly.

Storage decisions are ongoing, because household needs inevitably change as family needs evolve. But once there's a storage plan, revising it periodically should not be difficult. Take inspiration from what inventive designers and homeowners have done, as pictured in *Store It!* Their work confirms that even the most practical storage solutions can be attractive and appealing.

—MERVYN KAUFMAN

1 ENTRANCE CUES

MUDROOMS AND ENTRY HALLS are busy, high-traffic areas in almost any house. An entry hall, which could be a narrow widening inside the front door or a very formal foyer, is the first thing you and your guests notice upon entering your home. Making it neat as well as functional is an enviable goal and can be an organizational challenge.

A mudroom is where boots and outerwear are shed, shopping bags get dropped, and keys and coins are tossed. Coats, hats, schoolbags, umbrellas, and often shoes are left out in the open, creating visual chaos—and making it hard to find what you need to deal with or wear. People tend to give lip service to the idea of providing efficient storage in these spaces—places to store what comes into the house or what must be grabbed or donned on the way out. Of course, what often happens is that eventually the messiness becomes less visible. You may not see it anymore unless you happen to trip on it.

A glass-paneled patio door opens into a spacious entry (opposite) whose mottled brick floor adds a note of rusticity to a refined ambience. On a wall of built-ins, floor-to-ceiling storage includes six easy-gliding drawers plus three floor-to-ceiling closets. Facing that wall system is an oversize chest with storage drawers below and wall hooks directly above.

When space is tight, creativity takes over. In a tiny hall corner (top), staggered hooks hold hats, coats, and scarves; tin trays are aligned to hold shoes and contain outdoor mud; umbrellas reside in a tall stand. A bamboo coat rack with its own sensible-height mirror (above) is a convenient catchall for various handbags and hats.

FIRST IMPRESSIONS

Pretend you are a first-time visitor to your home. Go outside and re-enter via the front door. Stand in the foyer or front hall and look around. What do you see? Is there a place to plunk a folded umbrella, a surface on which to rest a briefcase, handbag, or tote? Is there enough light to make the space feel cheery and welcoming? And if there's a closet, does it have rack space not only for your family's off-season outerwear but also for guest coats and cold-weather gear? Equally important, is the space generally free of clutter?

DESIGNER SUGGESTIONS Pros agree that keeping clutter under control can be liberating, but it also makes demands. Jerome Currie Hanauer, a New York City designer, tackles the problem head-on: "You have to take a hard look at everything—decide what you need to keep and what you can toss." For him, some degree of paring down must occur first, before any of the following storage solutions are even considered:

- Instead of a hall table, consider a small chest or a console table with at least one drawer. Keeping items in drawers rather than out in the open is a practical, effective way to create an uncluttered look.

- Provide a place for everything likely to be dropped on any flat surface: a bowl or basket for keys, sunglasses, and mail, for example, plus a tall container for wet umbrellas. Don't clutter an entry with family photos; display them in the family room or in a hall leading to your bedrooms.

- Make sure your guest closet really is that. While it may be a great place to store infrequently used or off-season clothing, be sure to reserve space on the rod for guest coats, and ditch those wire hangers. Keep a clutch of wooden hangers on hand to add to the feeling of welcome.

- Decorate your guest closet as you would any room: Apply wallpaper, a fresh coat of paint, some shelf liner, and perhaps some shelf trim.

DECORATIVE SPACE-STRETCHERS If space in your home is limited, it's possible to make a hall or entry do double duty without making it feel less welcoming.

- Splurge on an attractive piece of storage furniture with drawers and shelves for caps, gloves, and scarves. If an electrical outlet is handy, this could also be a recharging station for portable electronic gear.

- If your guest closet has shelves, you can store seasonal items there if you label the containers "Summer," "Winter," "Fall," or "Spring."

Refinished and its drawers removed, an old desk (above) is ideal small-foyer furniture. Mailing tubes and colorful letter boxes hold catalogs and mail; winter gear is at home in the wicker cube; umbrellas have a special place to stand and drip; and wall hooks hold leashes and the occasional hat. In this rear entry (left), a stable coat rack has its own sunlit corner, but the antique bench, with storage drawers and open space for boots and shoes, is the focus.

A BUSY BACK ENTRANCE

CONVENIENCE AND PRACTICALITY If properly equipped and decorated, a mudroom can give a house an effective transition between interior and exterior spaces. When planning or organizing a mudroom, think carefully about how your family is likely to use the space. Will groceries come in through the back door? If so, you may want to include a shelf or counter to rest bags on after unloading the car.

MATERIAL CHOICES Mudrooms tend to take a lot of abuse. When starting from scratch, select durable, low-maintenance products— easily laid, mop-able sheet linoleum on the floor, for example. Newest examples come in a huge variety of colors and patterns and, as linoleum is produced from natural materials, it is environmentally friendly.

An idea worth considering is beadboard wainscoting, which has an appealing texture and is more resistant to scratches and dings than painted wallboard. Here are other suggestions:

- A bench is a must, particularly one with space underneath for shoe or boot storage—either in open niches or pull-out baskets.

- A desirable alternative is a bench with storage space hidden beneath a hinged lift-up seat.

- Position one or more low shelf units around the room, and assign a specific theme to each one. Kids' crafts could be one; garden supplies might be another.

- A waist- or chest-high storage unit will include a top shelf that could be a likely source of clutter. If you keep that surface pretty clear, it can double as a work station as well as a place for grocery bags, book bags, and totes.

Built-in shelving lines both walls of a long entrance hall (above), which draws the eye to a living room whose soaring stone fireplace is its centerpiece. Family treasures and books are neatly displayed, row by row, in niches, but generous space exists in each one, so there is never a hint of overcrowding.

- Turn your mudroom into a recycling center—not for kitchen waste but as a central location for the many other no-longer-needed items that a household may accumulate. You could stack old newspapers in an opaque plastic bin (available at home centers), then be sure to keep tie-up twine handy in a small wicker tray.

- Hang keys to the house, cars, and bike locks in a small wooden cabinet mounted on the wall near the back door. When the cabinet door is open, each key is visible; when closed, the unit is a decorative accent.

- If there is room, consider purchasing new or secondhand steel lockers, which can provide closed storage for items you don't want displayed.

- Set down a small rubber or plastic mat to collect mud from shoes and wet boots. A large flat basket would be a decorative alternative.

- Keep pet gear and cleaning supplies out of sight by placing wood or plastic bins or wicker baskets under an open bench.

SPORTS STORY The mudroom, like the traditional service porch that preceded it, is often a dumping ground for kids' sports gear. If handled properly, this equipment can be stored without cluttering.

- Built-in shelves or niches can inspire neatness, if it is obvious that every item—helmets, balls, bats, jackets—has its own place.

- Create a defined space for each young family member. It should have hooks, cubbies or drawers, shelves or cupboards, and a nameplate.

- Reinforce the concept of pride of possession: Make each child feel responsible for maintaining his or her labeled storage spaces.

This multiuse entry (above) has one wall devoted to an upholstered bench, with storage units above, below, and to one side. The opposite wall (left) is a drop zone where cell phones can be recharged. The cabinet has drawers for bill storage, open shelves for attractive containers, and one tall cupboard for outerwear.

- Make your mudroom a true transition space, a place where items just delivered or hauled in from the car can be dropped, if only temporarily, and items about to be loaded into the car can rest, awaiting further action. Enclosed storage, built-in or freestanding, will work for stashing items temporarily, keeping everything in one contained area.

- Make neatness your watchword. Whether the objects are kept in cupboards, cabinets, or closets—or in cubbyholes or on open shelves— an orderly arrangement will eliminate sloppiness and also make it infinitely easier to find and access whatever you have stored.

DECORATING FOR UTILITY

There is no reason why a utilitarian, all-purpose space like a mudroom cannot also be an attractive space to be in, even if you are just passing through. Your front hall or foyer may be a kind of ultra decorating showcase—making that all-important first impression on visitors and guests. Conversely, your back hall or mudroom is probably the space that family members use most often, in their daily comings and goings. But there is no reason why it cannot be well lit, painted or wallpapered in a cheery fashion, and made to feel welcoming, too, even for the youngsters who may dash in and out repeatedly during the course of a day.

With its huge storage capacity, a modest-size mudroom (above) holds boots, cleaning needs, and sports and recycling gear. Equally efficient is a super-size mudroom (above, left), with hooks for clothing and totes, cubbies for sports gear, and baskets for small items. The corner seat has room for more than one person to change shoes and boots. Wall hooks carry the day in a paneled mudroom (opposite). The battered bench, two rows of hooks, and a mop-able floor make this a real workhorse area.

EXPERT IDEAS Donald W. Powers, AIA, a Rhode Island–based architect, has an informal approach to organizing mudroom storage. "Don't try too hard to give every item its own place," he advises. "A perfectly composed mudroom, with color-coordinated bins for everything, requires too much effort to maintain. Instead, make spaces and storage options that, even if they don't give everything its own home, at least give it a neighborhood." Here are other Powers points to consider:

- It is important for family members to have their own general zones: "Rather than keeping all the coats in one place and all the boots and shoes in another, for example, give each family member a cubby with room for all of his or her things." His hope is that all in the family will be responsible for their individual areas, thus increasing the chances that the mudroom can always stay organized.

Despite its casual theme, this spacious mudroom (above) really means business. Hammered-iron hardware on vibrant green cabinet doors adds timeless charm, yet within the cabinets most of a family's storage and entertaining needs are satisfied. A working sink is a bonus, as is the long wooden bench with boot storage under it.

- Defining a spot where stuff can accumulate without seeming out of control will let the mudroom function well even when it is not at its neatest.

- Build in catchall storage to stash the vacuum cleaner when you can't get it back to its cupboard or empty boxes until your next trip to the garage recycling area.

CLOSET CULTURE If your mudroom has the luxury of a closet, many of your storage needs in this area of your home can be accommodated. Here, if properly arranged and appointed, there will be a rod to hold outerwear on hangers. Why not add a second rod at a lower level for youngsters to use? If a rod with its own supply of hangers is provided, perhaps the kids themselves will opt for neatness.

- If the closet has one or more overhead shelves, they can be designated for storing specific items—sports gear in cartons or packaged trash bags.

- You might also consider bringing in a low, narrow chest with drawers that can hold gloves, mittens, and caps—accessible to everyone in the family.

- Don't neglect the back of the closet door. You might not do this in your foyer—where any hint of clutter should be discouraged—but in a back hall or mudroom, why not mount hooks inside the door to hold backpacks, bicycle helmets, softball mitts, and maybe an assortment of balls in a string bag hung on a sturdy hook?

FURNITURE Lacking a closet, you will have to bring in your own mudroom storage. But considering how many stock cabinets and shelf units in various sizes are available at home centers, this should not be challenging.

- Before going out to shop, and certainly before buying anything, draw up a mudroom plan, to scale, if possible. Show where windows and doors exist—they cut into potential wall space—then see where you might position a tall cupboard, floor-to-ceiling series of cubbies, or one or more shelf units where baskets or boxes could be stashed.

- Some seating here is essential, but it need not be a bench. If there is insufficient room, a simple chair will suffice, as long as everyone in your family is prepared to wait their turn.

- Whether you have built-ins or freestanding pieces, make sure the hooks, cubbies, shelves, and drawers are adequate for family needs.

Just inside a front door is a combination mudroom (above)—with upholstered seating, a mirror, and a deep cupboard for boots—and fully stocked message center. Frosted-glass cabinet doors keep visible the shapes and colors inside the lighted cabinets. Open shelves hold office gear. The quartz countertop is a wipeable writing and work surface.

2 | WELCOMING SPACES

THE LIVING ROOM IS A RELIC. At least that's what so many trend-watchers want people to believe. Yes, it's probably smaller than it once was, and many of its functions have been supplanted by the great room, which may include kitchen and dining room, and also by the family room. Even so, the living room is alive and well.

The family room is most homes' inevitable gathering spot. It tends to be informal, casual, and so loose in the way it's used that clutter and chaos abound. In short, it's inevitably a dumping ground for everything from books to board games, new DVDs to old newspapers.

Last rites were performed on the dining room back in the '80s, but that room still exists, even in homes with breakfast rooms and eat-in kitchens. Of course, some dining rooms do double duty as libraries and music rooms, which suggests that books and CDs are stored along with crystal, silver, family china, and collectibles.

Here is one way to add practical storage to an airy, open living room (opposite). Angled toward the window is a hand-painted hutch that lends classic warmth and elegance to an essentially cool decorating scheme. Behind the cabinet's closed doors are shelves for trays and serving pieces; the drawers hold coasters and cocktail napkins.

LIVING ROOMS

The 21st-century living room evolved from the 19th-century parlor, which was likely to be formal, somewhat stiff, and used only on special occasions. It also had a reputation for being dark, insulated— removed from the outside world as well as the rest of the house. Today's living room, though often still a special-occasion spot, is likely to be integrated seamlessly into the design of the rest of the house. As such, it must carry some of the household's need for storage.

SUBTLE INCLUSIONS As a welcoming space, the living room should always appear uncluttered, which means that storage should be, if not invisible, then certainly understated, with nothing to mar an overall sense of serenity. But serene need not mean stuffy. A living room should appear...*livable*. And bright. As New York interior designer Bruce Bierman says, "I like a room to always feel well lit."

Comfortable contemporary-style seating is arranged around the giant restored vintage fireplace mantel in a living room designed for collectors (below). In shelving that flanks French doors that open out to a patio, much of the owners' collection of fine-art pottery is displayed. Confined to these two areas, its impact is maximal, and none of it creates a feeling of clutter in the space.

DISPLAY AND VISIBILITY

A living room is the ideal place to display family treasures, small works of art, and valuable crafts and ceramic pieces. Arranged on shelves or behind glass doors, they become vivid expressions of a family's taste and interests.

- Built-ins are usually the perfect places for storing and displaying objects, particularly if their design coordinates with the style and scale of your room.

- Harness wall space in corners, between windows, and even under windows, depending on the way your living room is laid out. Built-ins take minimal room and, without overwhelming the space, can provide you with as much open and closed storage as you may require.

- If investing in built-in storage pieces, focus on the idea of storage as furniture. Woodwork trim should mimic the room's crown moldings or the decorative design of a fireplace mantel. The idea is to make your built-ins part of the living room's interior architecture.

- Color should play a large part in the treatment of the built-ins you choose. In most rooms, built-in furniture repeats the room's overall color theme—either the wall tone or the color chosen for all of the wood trim. What designer Bierman favors is not color contrast but monotone. "The subtlety," he says, "comes through the fact that everything is the same color."

- No matter how proud you are of whatever you collect, consider holding back. Don't put everything you own on shelves. Keep some items in reserve, and rotate them periodically—perhaps seasonally—to keep a constantly fresh look. Your family will appreciate the frequent changes, as will even the guests who visit you often. Familiarity can be boring.

Storage shelves made to measure between two tall windows (above) make this wall the decorating focal point of a country living room. The display shelves are mounted above bookshelves on either side of the house's original working steam-heat radiator. What makes the display so striking, despite the fact that it contains mostly low-cost flea-market finds, is that all but a few of the collected pieces are stark white.

Asian elegance adds texture to this high-ceilinged living room (above). Set in front of a tall, curved, silver-leafed niche on which an artist has painted a flowering tree is a bow-front console that holds many examples of the blue-and-white porcelains the owners collect. The display changes often; with replacements close at hand, rotating pieces is easy to do and remember.

STORAGE IN DISGUISE Especially in living rooms, where a clean, uncluttered look is an important and much-sought-after goal, pieces of furniture can lead double lives—not only as components of an overall decorating scheme but as places to stash or display things.

- A console can be an attractive focus in a living room; it can also be a significant, though limited, source of storage. You won't want to cram toys or games behind its delicate doors, but you could keep vases, urns, spare hors d'oeuvres platters, and any other items you like to keep close at hand when hosting guests. Best advice: Store in a console only those items that you plan to use or display in your living room.

- If new furniture is on your list of living room needs, once you have selected seating and determined where to place it, think in broad terms about the case goods you will need to complete the setting. As storage in a living room is usually limited, and certainly should be, every piece of case-goods furniture you consider bringing in should include space where you can put things.

- For decorating impact as well as storage capacity, look for furniture that contains a mix: open shelves as well as drawers, for example, and drawers as well as cupboards. This kind of variety is useful and highly functional; it can also provide additional visual interest.

- The coffee table may not be the most important piece of furniture in a living room, but as it is usually positioned prominently, and often centrally, it does get a lot of attention. Yes, the top is a logical spot for a bowl of flowers or a lazy Susan with saucers of dip. But think how much more useful it would be if it there was a shelf or a row of shallow drawers under that convenient top. The shelves could hold elegant books or magazines; the drawers, coasters and cocktail napkins.

- End tables are often placed at either end of a sofa or love seat—perfect places for table lamps that add subtle illumination and also make it possible for someone seated there to read. But when storage space is at a premium, narrow table-height chests—with drawers and maybe one open shelf—are very often acceptable, space-conscious additions.

- When shopping for storage-capacity end tables, keep in mind the scale of your living room and the usable space at each end of your seating. You will want to look for furniture that complements the decorating style of your room; in addition, you will want to seek out grace rather than bulk.

- Books, like collectibles, can be displayed in a living room, but only in a limited fashion. Be choosy; place books of similar size and bulk in small clusters; don't fill an entire shelf—leave breathing room. Or add a piece of pottery to the end of a shelf. Books and collectibles make an interesting juxtaposition.

- Use surfaces sparingly. A bowl of fruit or flowers plus a short stack of books may be all you need to complete the look of your coffee table; a single object beside a lamp may be just what an end table needs; a few objects arranged on a mantel or the top of a console or an occasional table can provide a dollop of interest without cluttering the space.

Built-in cabinets, each with two folding recessed-panel doors, flank the Federal-style fireplace centered on the wall (below). Each cabinet has shelves for books, games, and electronic gear. The cabinet shown, which rises to window height, is also equipped to hold a flat-screen TV and a music system, turning this living room into a comfortable, inviting home-entertainment center.

DINING ROOMS

DISAPPEARING GRANDEUR There was a time when dining room doorways were adorned with imaginary velvet ropes, as these were rooms to be used only on formal occasions—that is, when company came. As social morés began to change, the classic dining room began to lose its stuffy stature. Schoolkids found the table the best place for spreading out their homework, and many a school project or family craft project was executed on the dining table's long, wide surface. Then, of course, dining rooms began to merge with other rooms. There were living-dining rooms, kitchen-dining rooms, and great rooms with dining tables stuck in one corner. The reason: People could no longer devote a single enclosed space to a rarely occurring event like a holiday dinner. If a dining room existed, it had to serve more than one master.

Arts and Crafts–style pendants add soft light and underscore the early 20th-century theme of this high-ceilinged dining room (below). A tall antique vitrine, placed in the corner beside a door to the kitchen, stores and displays some of the owners' collectibles behind wood-framed doors with glass insets.

- A wall of books—either in made-to-measure built-in shelf units or nearly ceiling-high furniture with generous shelving—can effectively enrich the design of most dining rooms without compromising their purpose as a place for formal dining.

- Hutches, sideboards, and breakfronts add stylish touches and also supply the hidden storage that every dining room needs. Depending on the size of the room, its furnishings should include cupboards for china and serving pieces, plus drawers for silverware and important serving utensils—each drawer fitted out with dividers so forks, knives, and spoons can be accessed easily.

- Yes, a wonderful heirloom coffee service deserves to be put on display—right in the center of the dining table, on top of the sideboard, or on a deep shelf. But china coffee cups and saucers may be safer if stacked neatly on a shelf inside a closed cupboard.

■ Lighting often limits the flexibility of the traditional dining room. That chandelier hanging from the middle of the ceiling virtually dictates the placement of the dining table, which in turn pretty much determines where all the other furnishings, including storage, will be positioned.

■ When redoing a dining room, think of replacing the chandelier with a series of appropriately spaced recessed ceiling fixtures that will provide even illumination in every area of the room. Dimmer switches will make it possible to adjust the lighting levels—medium to low for candlelit dining, medium to high for game playing or completing homework assignments. Sconces are another option. They can be either traditional or contemporary, depending on room style.

■ Another boon to flexibility is the old-fashioned tea cart. It stands on wheels and once stood in the corner of great-grandmother's dining room. But it didn't stand alone. There may have been a tea service arranged on it or one or more stacks of dessert plates, and on special occasions, perhaps, too, a vase of fresh flowers; thus it was not only attractive but also useful. Flexible, too. Move it around and it became an excellent aid to serving a meal. Our forebears knew the secret.

Striking in its simplicity though massive in scale, a door-height cabinet (above) has shelves, drawers, and cupboards that contain all dining room essentials in one convenient place. The piece sets a contemporary tone for the space, just as the spare amount of white ceramic pieces that dot the open shelves defines a cool, uncluttered environment.

BREAKFAST BONUSES In our wickedly fast-paced society, a great many people, including students as well as working people, gobble breakfast on the run. It's not very nourishing, thus not very healthy. Many of these quick diners are not so much in a rush as less than eager to transfer their breakfast fixings from the kitchen to a table that may be in another room. There was a time, of course, when the average household had a breakfast room, which was utilized daily, as well as a dining room, the site of evening and holiday meals. When kitchen counters were expanded to include space for snack and breakfast dining, the breakfast room just about disappeared. Then the pendulum swung back. Yes, kitchen islands and peninsulas have dining zones, but many a new home also includes a sizable space for informal dining. Whether it is only used in the morning or for all family dining, it is still called a breakfast room.

- Whether the breakfast room is an extension of the kitchen or a room adjacent to it, its style should reflect that of the rest of the house.

- The ideal breakfast room not only has a table and enough chairs for all in the family, it also has storage— for everyday tableware, flatware, and serving pieces, all of which would otherwise sap some of the kitchen's precious storage space.

- Separating meal preparation from meal serving will reduce traffic flow in the kitchen as well as clutter. If a child in the family is asked to set the breakfast table, he or she can perform the chore without being underfoot.

- Since this is a family space, attractive plates can crowd the walls and other collectibles can be spread on other surfaces.

Storage is a subtle presence in this French country–style dining room (opposite). Drawers in the old farmhouse table hold flatware; other serving essentials are kept in drawers in the Shaker-style chest that stands against the wall. Modest in scale and bulk, this long-legged console in a dining room (below) is a handy place to store table linens and flatware.

It may look like hardly more than a raised coffee table placed in front of the high-backed sofa in this multi-windowed family room (above), but the antique steamer trunk with its gleaming brass hardware has enormous storage capacity. Open it, and inside are usable shelves and niches for games, CDs, DVDs, and books. When closed, it provides a smooth-top surface for serving snacks, drinks, and nibbles.

FAMILY ROOMS

PRACTICAL AND FLEXIBLE The family room, which used to be the den and is now sometimes one section of the great room, is a multipurpose high-traffic space. People lounge there, watch TV shows and DVDs, and listen to music. Children play games, scatter their toys, and entertain friends there. Since it gets so much varied use, it requires a lot of storage, because unless it stays organized, a family room can become chaotic and off-putting, a kind of household no-man's-land. The secret to organizing this much-used space is storage appropriate to what you want to keep there.

- Before buying or building storage facilities, take the measure of what you need—literally. Use a tape measure and note how much shelf space will be required for books, toys, games, CDs, DVDs, and all the various entertainment aids that family rooms acquire.

- Keep in mind that even if your family room lacks room enough for a table for snack dining, family members will inevitably bring food there.

So keep flat surfaces relatively bare, to make sure that food scraps don't land between seat, sofa, or chair cushions. Tabletop surfaces here should be strictly utilitarian—wipeable and stain resistant.

- Consider freestanding storage units here. As family needs change, you will want to rearrange your furniture rather than having to replace it.

- Organize what needs to be stored according to where it will be used: near the TV, beside the music system, in what you decide the kids' play area will be, in a quiet corner reserved for reading. Having a large family room will net you little unless the space is used wisely.

- Seek out and use spaces that are often overlooked: Corners are an excellent spot for bookcases; the back of a floating sofa is ideal for placing a long, low bookshelf; a cupboard built under a window seat can be a great receptacle for spare pillows and throws.

- No matter how big it is, a family room never has enough space, so think of multipurpose pieces: an antique steamer trunk that could be a handsome centerpiece and also an excellent place to store games

Closed cabinets below a raised fireplace give the far wall of this large family room (top) dual functions. Cushions flanking the fireplace opening provide soft bench seating. Shallow shelving and deep ledges (above) add needed storage benefits to a contemporary family room fireplace design. Niches and a wide ledge built into an expanded mantel (left) create display niches for books, framed pictures, and family treasures.

or blankets; an ottoman whose top lifts up to reveal generous storage space inside.

DESIGNER SUGGESTIONS "I think it's best not to have lots of furniture but to have a few large pieces that can hold a lot of things," advises Ann Gordinier, a Seattle-based interior designer. Here are some of her other ideas for making a family room a super storage zone:

- Even if there are things kept in the family room that you tend to use often, find places to put them. "The idea is to keep things off of most surfaces," she says.

- To ensure that you can create order in this clutter-prone space, she favors an armoire: "If you opt for one, make sure it has a space big enough to hold your TV, plus drawers for videotapes, DVDs, and CDs, and shelves for books."

- Gordinier explains why she has a strong preference for bookcases: "They hold many more items besides books that can otherwise clutter your tabletops, chests, and desks."

- As not every item of recurring use will have a suitable place in a drawer or on a shelf, at least one alternative is possible: "Baskets," says Gordinier. "They can hold reading glasses and the remote controls for your TV, DVD player, and stereo."

- "If you like family photos to be visible, maximize their impact by displaying them in a single place," she urges.

- One way to do that: "Find ready-made ledges in various lengths at home centers or through a mail-order source. They are usually no more than two inches deep with a lip on top, perfect for propping a row of small picture frames," she suggests. "Mount the ledges on one wall or one section of a wall, so all of your photos are clustered together. Then, to avoid a dizzy look, choose frames in the same style and finish."

Storage and display needs go hand in hand in furniture of any period designed to be functional as well as decorative. Here (above), the double-duty reproduction side table and matching étagère behind an amply scaled armchair provide storage and display potential set against the pale purple wall of an antiques-filled family room.

SAVVY SPACE STRETCHERS

Because of its acceptably casual look, the family room can be a bit more cluttered than most other spaces in your home. But when selecting storage units, be sure to account for bonus space—to make room for items you may acquire in the future. If you plan to install your TV here, whether it sits on a shelf or in a cabinet, or is hung on the wall, make note of its dimensions. Here are ways to utilize family room space in an optimal way:

- Arrange furniture so that the room's various functions can be separated: dining, lounging, game-playing, reading.

- Use a freestanding bookcase to create a functional divider between a reading corner and the rest of the room.

- Mounting the TV on a wall is a good way to save valuable family room space. But doing so may limit the room's flexibility. If you prefer to keep options open, why not put your TV on a bench or a low cabinet, one topping either storage shelves or drawers? An entertainment center is another option, but keep in mind that when you want to use the TV, you'll have to open cabinet doors and *hope* that what's stored inside is arranged neatly, not a jumbled mess.

- Floor-to-ceiling bookshelves reach their potential by co-opting leftover space above and around doors. Books and other objects that are used infrequently can create an appealing display on the topmost berth.

- A wall-mounted lamp will eliminate the need for a table, or will liberate a tabletop for use holding myriad other items.

- Don't overlook the wall space under windows. A window seat can easily double as a storage unit—fitted with either drawers or a hinged top—and requires a minimum depth of 22 inches for seating comfort.

A frame within a frame within a frame: At one end of an urban family room (above), display niches are arranged around a tall mirror, itself elegantly framed, hung within the largest opening. With its built-in look, this custom piece has great flexibility, and because the mirror is prominent, it also creates a feeling of expanded space.

A giant TV dominates this sunny family room (above), but the unit doesn't stand alone. It's tucked into a custom unit that includes closed cupboards—to store all of the household's entertaining needs—plus shelves for books, framed pictures, and collectibles on display.

MEDIA ROOMS

The ideal media room would have comfortable seating—armchairs and sofas—in a theater-like arrangement. The TV would be sized perfectly to the scale of the room, and wall-mounted or built-in speakers would be placed appropriately to achieve a surround-sound effect. And, of course, the walls would be soundproofed so that no household sounds would disturb the occupants. Not every household has the luxury of having a single room so dedicated. Thus, the media room is often part of a den or one corner of a family room—places where separation is implied rather than realized. You can create a visual separation through a skillful arrangement of furniture; you can also make this shared space somewhat independent by providing sufficient storage for everything that is usually utilized there.

STOW THE GEAR The CDs, DVDs, and videotapes that are likely to be left on tables or scattered around are perhaps the greatest source of clutter in media rooms or in any parts of a home dedicated to home entertainment. Jennifer Humes, a Dallas-based home organizer, and Andrea Rideout of Garland, Texas, whose *Ask Andrea* airs on several hundred radio stations around the country, offer these media room storage suggestions:

- Whether you decide to stow your gear on open shelves or in closed cupboards, make a point of keeping children's-interest tapes and discs at lower levels, grownups' stuff higher up.

- Alphabetize your film library for easy access. Mix videotapes and DVDs, so you don't have to search for movies in two different places.

- If space is tight, consider acquiring a four-sided revolving CD tower that can be tucked in a corner or kept in a closet. Within its small footprint, a storage tower can hold a film library as well as recorded music.

- If you prefer hiding your entertainment inventory, consider shelving with doors or a freestanding armoire. Label the edge of each interior shelf with the genre or category, so that items get put back in the right place after use. Tip: Buy an inexpensive label maker so the labels you create have a standard look and are attractive as well as readable.

- Color-code labels so that even the youngest members of the family can identify the music, TV shows, or films they want to play.

- If your shelving is deep enough, you can layer what you store: Place seldom-played discs and tapes behind those you reach for often.

- To minimize storage space for CDs and DVDs, toss the cases and retain only the discs. One disc, plus liner notes, can be slipped into a clear-acrylic pocket and stashed in a loose-leaf binder. A binder with 50 sheets can hold up to 200 discs, a good-size home library.

To conserve space and organize storage efficiently within much-used family rooms, two wall units (top and left) combine book and collectible storage in large-scale pieces, each with a place for a TV. Ottomans are known for their flexibility—as bonus seating as well as footrests. Here (above), an ottoman with a cleverly hinged top provides storage space for pillows and throws.

3 | CATCHALL KITCHENS

LIVING, COOKING, DINING, and entertaining styles are major factors in determining how a kitchen should be designed and laid out. All of these factors converge in any discussion of storage. Are there two or more cooks in your household, or just one? Do you like to entertain guests in your kitchen, or prefer cooking and entertaining to remain wholly separate? Do you prefer an eat-in kitchen, or would you rather serve snacks and casual meals in an adjacent space? *Space.* That's the kicker. You can never have too much of it, right? Of course. But even more important than having enough is how it is used. Maximized. Not wasted. As you will see, it's possible to squeeze plenty of storage into even a modest-size kitchen. The key is knowing how much you want to store—even before you set out to buy or add the gear. The challenge then becomes how to utilize your storage facilities fully and, at the same time, ensure that they fulfill all of your kitchen needs.

Windows flood this kitchen (opposite) with sunlight but limit wall space for storage. To compensate, shelving and cabinetry are custom-fitted to a wall between windows; deep drawers stack on either side of the range; and the island provides drawers and cupboards along with the work surface, undermount sink, and warming drawer.

THE EVOLVING KITCHEN

It wasn't too long ago that the kitchen was a sterile space at the back of the house that only the cook and her helpers (yes, the home cook was traditionally female) entered and worked in. Then, with lifestyle changes, nearly everyone in the family developed some kind of cooking skill, and kitchen design reflected that. The kitchen became a magnet, and as home design began to deconstruct, the strict and very formal living room–dining room–kitchen arrangement gradually loosened. Today, kitchens tend to be open spaces that flow into other rooms in the house, and people entertain in their kitchens even more often than they once did in their living and dining rooms. When walls came down, storage needs became—and remain—challenging.

STORAGE STRATEGIES Determining your actual storage requirements is fairly undemanding. Start by making a list of everything you store or plan to store in your kitchen. Then do an inventory of what you

The top row of cabinets in a U-shaped kitchen (below) has glass-inset doors, which add interest and dimension to a crisp, white space. There is also a functional bonus: Seldom-used items are stored high up but are always visible, so no one has to ponder what lies within each hard-to-reach space.

have. Compile your inventory by category, grouping items you prefer to keep together—spices, condiments, and cooking oils, for example. Measure the tallest and shortest items, so you can make sure the storage accessories you buy will mesh with your drawer and shelf dimensions.

- Consider usage, separating items in daily use from those in rare or occasional use. You will probably want to store often-used items somewhere between knee height and eye level, right where you work; lesser-used items, in more distant locations.

- Keep in mind the way you tend to function. How do your shopping and cooking routines affect your storage? Do you buy food in bulk all at once, or do you prefer to shop frequently, on demand? And how often do you or others in your family prepare meals at home?

- While examining everything you keep in your kitchen, begin to do some positive weeding out. Are there packages or jars you've never opened or rarely touched? If unopened, offer them to a friend or neighbor. If unsealed, don't be hesitant to simply throw them out.

CONVENIENCE VS. CLUTTER The key to a clutter-free kitchen is organization: where you put what you choose to store. If you are building a new kitchen or remodeling an existing one, consider cabinet layout as you develop a design. Best advice: Choose cabinets fitted with features and accessories that will make neatness second nature. Note that most cabinet models usually include an array of

Color change enriches the sleek design of a kitchen that overlooks a landscaped backyard (above). Cabinets and shelves rise to ceiling height, and a strip of cabinets with glass fronts and backs provides storage without interrupting the flow of natural light. Essential cookware hangs from an industrial ceiling rack.

organizing options that can markedly augment kitchen efficiency. No matter who does the family cooking, storing tools and utensils near where they are most frequently needed is a principal strategy.

- Exploit a wall. Attach a heavy-duty rail system along the backsplash and mount a rack on it for frequently used spices and condiments. Or hang your favorite cooking utensils or a cookbook holder there.

- Compartmentalize. A wide-open space can be an invitation to chaos. Dividers and other organizers placed in cupboards and drawers will help you find a proper home for everything you own.

- Capture corners. Increasingly sophisticated design has made space in corner base cabinets more accessible, thus much more usable.

Shaker simplicity punctuated with Art Nouveau accents makes this kitchen (opposite) an elegant place to entertain as well as cook. By contrast, Arts and Crafts curves and tapers (below) define a kitchen designed for storage as well as style. Closed cabinets above the refrigerator-freezer and an adjacent ceiling-high pantry conceal the basics—salad bowls, trays, and cookie sheets—along with multiple shelves for packaged foods. Open shelves and glass-fronted cabinets display handsome tableware and serving pieces. Cookware has a spacious home in drawers positioned beside the range.

Hand-rubbed, red-painted maple cabinets are not the only designed-in element requested by homeowners who dared not to be neutral. Storage was a key requirement, realized by (left, top to bottom) a handy small-appliance garage; a two-drawer dishwasher hidden behind cabinet fronts; retractable dishtowel bars that fill otherwise unused space; a corner base cabinet with shelving attached to its pull-out door; plus (below) open shelves for a handsome display, accessible hooks for often-used utensils, and a hutch-wide plate rack above small, shallow cutlery drawers and a butcher-block work surface.

Crowded but uncluttered, this kitchen
(above) displays what the homeowners
like to use and collect, including an
old painted bench. More cautious but
equally compelling is a remodeled
kitchen (right) that features open
shelving instead of wall cabinets, plus
storage in bin-handled cabinets and
drawers. A recessed wall with three deep
shelves for often-used items (opposite,
top left) was designed for storage
along with a waist-height microwave,
under-cabinet beverage coolers, and a
bar sink. Rough-hewn beams echo the
informality of open shelving in a country
kitchen (opposite, top right). Flanked
by bracket-hung shelves, wire racks
(opposite, bottom) are mounted against
the steel backsplash under a kitchen's
steel range hood.

ACCESSIBILITY PLUS VISIBILITY Glass-fronted wall units break up the mass of a run of closed cabinets and also allow you to keep an eye on items you regularly need. Whether paneled with transparent or frosted glass, these doors will reinforce the desire for neatness. Here are other aids to maintaining order in this hub of home activity:

■ Slide-out baskets—either designed to reside in a base cabinet or freestanding on a cabinet shelf—are a great way to store vegetables and fruit, even bread. Basket storage will allow these fresh foods to breathe but also stay off the countertop and out of the way until needed.

■ Stow spatulas and other workhorse utensils in a ceramic or steel canister beside your cooktop or range. The tools will be more accessible here, and drawer space can be reserved for items used less often.

■ Putting pots and pans on hooks suspended from a ceiling rack—hung over a work island or a cooking appliance—will make them easier to reach when you are in the midst of meal prep or are actually cooking.

■ An appliance garage, with a space-saving tambour door that rolls up—out of sight—and then down for a concealed look is a good place to keep a toaster and coffeemaker. If an electrical connection can be installed, these appliances can be used without ever moving them.

A stainless steel shelf hung above the range (below) puts essential cooking gear in the center spotlight. Making every surface count—and carry more than its usual weight—was the mandate for designers of a tiny galley kitchen (right). A knife rack hung on the end of one wall cabinet, a top row of glass-fronted cabinets, and two-tier revolving carousel shelving in the corner of L-shaped base cabinetry complete the storage picture.

STORAGE STRETCHERS Every kitchen has wasted spaces—places where a shelf, a rack, or a shallow drawer could be tucked. Finding and using these bonus spaces will help keep a kitchen functioning smoothly as well as clutter-free, no matter how big or small it is.

■ Instead of stacking pots and pans on shelves in base cabinets, where some are likely to be pushed back—out of sight—consider placing cookware, lids and all, in deep drawers near your cooking appliances.

■ Make the most of corner base cabinets. Cookware tends to get buried deep in corner recesses, so why not explore one of these possibilities: carousel shelves that revolve at the touch or swing-out shelving that reveals every item stored in a cabinet. Each of these easily installed accessories is available at home centers or big-box retailers.

■ Cabinet space in front of kitchen sinks is generally wasted, because it remains unused. Consider having a shallow tilt-out drawer installed there, one suitable for stowing sponges and other small-scale cleaning supplies.

Playing against scale—a tall, narrow window above an ultra-wide vintage sink—two sets of open shelves and a row of base cabinets (above) make the cleanup zone of an expanded kitchen a convenient place to work. An open corner wall cabinet (left) flanked by narrow glass-fronted cabinets makes the most of what would have been wasted space between a set of windows.

- Cabinets hung or placed above a refrigerator are often underutilized, relegated to storing miscellany. But if fitted out with tall dividers, for vertical tray, muffin-pan, or cookie-sheet storage, such units can become integral to a kitchen's efficient, space-saving work plan.

- Most cabinet doors swing out; in a small kitchen, they could become overhead hazards. An alternative is hinged cabinet doors that fold upward. These are usually designed to stay in the up position until a gentle pull brings them back down again...very slowly.

- Keep knives off the kitchen counter. If there is room, you can place them in a knife rack inside a base-cabinet drawer. Or use a magnetic holder hung on a meal-prep area wall or backsplash.

- A plate rack can be an attractive and accessible way to store large and small plates vertically, but some kitchens employ plate rails for platter display on an otherwise unused wall. Horizontal stack-ups are also possible—on open shelves or in deep drawers fitted with peg dividers.

In a sparkling contemporary kitchen behind an expansive window with a lush backyard view (opposite), a row of low steel cabinets on legs extends beneath that window and wraps around to the range wall. Drawer storage dominates base cabinets (left), and there is even a pair of shallow drawers tucked under the built-in microwave (above). Raise-up awning-style doors make upper cabinet contents less challenging to reach (bottom, far left), and a tall, narrow drawer near the far corner is a conveniently placed receptacle for recyclables (bottom, left).

HIDDEN ASSETS

SPECIAL SOLUTIONS Sometimes, solving a mystery means just looking a little harder—in this instance, at elements in the kitchen that may have escaped notice. The trick is to avoid adding anything if there is no extra room but make the most of what may already exist.

- A mixer or food processor need not hog counter space when not being used. A special cabinet insert makes it possible to raise the appliance to counter height for use, then return it to concealment thereafter.

- A narrow space between base cabinets need not go unutilized. A set of retractable towel bars will fit handily in a niche that can be kept open when towels need to dry, then closed when the dampness disappears.

- Your cutting board probably gets a daily workout, but it doesn't have to take valuable counter space when you're not using it. A pull-out drawer-style cutting board can be installed directly below countertop level, a location that is ergonomically superior to that of portable boards, which stand an inch or more above counter level. What makes the idea particularly appealing is the fact that the built-in board can be easily slid back into invisibility when its work is done.

A well-organized baking station (below), placed between the refrigerator and the sink, keeps tools and ingredients within arm's reach. A wide small-appliance garage, providing a home for both a mixer and processor, has a tambour door that can be rolled down when these appliances are not in use.

- Toekick space under a pantry cabinet, a drawer dishwasher, or a pair of wall ovens can be a useful storage plus—a convenient spot for pets' feeding bowls or a resting place for a folding stepladder that may be needed to reach the top shelves of ceiling-height cabinetry.

- Tap into a cabinet's inner secret spot: the door. It's easy to waste or overlook that space, but it could work well when there are skinny items to store: spice racks, pot-lid holders, or oven mitts hung on hooks.

- You can also mount storage racks on the back of the broom-closet door, or add shallow shelves to this closet's back wall to hold cleaning supplies.

BUDGET UPGRADES Eager to spruce up your kitchen but lack the means to fund an all-new installation? There are a number of ways to upgrade and update—to alter the look of your cabinets and the overall feel of your kitchen.

- Replace the solid wood doors of key wall cabinets with clear glass-paneled doors, then paint all of the exposed cabinet interiors a compelling contrast color.

- Instead of clear glass, opt for doors with frosted-glass insets, which will create a sense of openness without challenging your neatness instinct. From outside, colors and shapes will be evident, not details.

- Add architectural elements, such as ornate wood trim on upper cabinets, to dramatically alter the look of boxy stock construction.

- Remove some cabinet doors and allow stored items to be exposed and displayed on open shelving.

Bifold raise-up cabinet doors (above) ease the access to high-level storage. Frosted-glass door panels hide clutter but keep colors and shapes in soft focus so the cook knows what is kept where.

A long storage shelf extends high above an oversize French-made commercial range (above) in remodeled space that remains basically a galley kitchen. A row of earthenware crocks is arranged on that shelf, under which cast iron and gleaming copper cookware hang. Centerpiece of this kitchen's soaring storage wall (top, left) is a two-door pantry with pull-out open drawers and, at its center, rotating steel shelves designed for packaged products. To the right of the range are stainless steel shelves (center, left) sized to hold stacked bowls and covered pots. Divided drawers like this one (left) are deep enough for standing spice jars, bottled condiments, and folded cloth napkins.

- Sand, prime, and paint timeworn wood cabinets a daring primary color, then eliminate all other colorful kitchen accessories that would create contrast or compete for visual attention.

- Replace dated cabinet hardware. Choose trendy new handles and pulls, or those with an antique finish if you prefer a vintage look.

- Mount a pegboard panel on the back of a pantry or broom-closet door to hook-hang utensils, pots and pans, baskets, mops, or brooms.

- Attach a rack or bar for dishtowels at the end of an island or a long run of base cabinets.

- Insert a narrow cabinet or shelf unit in a wall between studs, creating a handy place to store canned or bottled products, even spices.

- If you have a worktable, whether it's new or old, you could add a lower shelf for colorful mixing bowls and oversize platters. You could even stash baskets filled with cooking staples, such as potatoes and onions.

- Scour local garage or tag sales for a small corner shelf unit that you can sand, stain, or repaint. Wall-hung or freestanding, it could become a decorative focus—a place to display attractive cups or plates, either of which would take valuable storage space elsewhere.

- Extend the depth of a kitchen windowsill to create a shelf where sun-loving herbs and other plants can be nurtured.

- Leave no wall space unused. If traffic flow is not impeded, why not mount open shelving where possible, and create additional places to store and display glassware, dishes, or some of your cookbooks?

- If you do add shelves, paint them the color of your kitchen trim or stain them to match, or complement, your cabinetry. Fronted with molding strips, these shelves can become part of kitchen furniture.

- Extend your island. Place a shallow counter-high cabinet at one or both ends, or at one end of a peninsula, to create a storage boost. If it's a flea market find that happens to fit, give it a contrasting finish; if it's an unfinished piece, paint or stain it to match your cabinets.

COOKBOOK DISPLAY Mount a hands-free recipe-book shelf near eye level above your range. Paint or stain it, and attach cabinet knobs just above it on either side. Link the knobs with a string tied tight, to hold the book in place. When not in use, open the book to a spread of pretty pictures and you'll have a rotating art display.

With handles enabling them to slide easily in and out of designed-in niches (above), four wicker baskets store fresh produce between two rows of cabinet drawers. Turned on its side, an antique garden gate (below) fitted out with lengths of pipe from a plumbing-supply store hangs from the vaulted ceiling of a kitchen with Asian accents. The gate itself, suspended above the range, serves as a shelf; cookware hangs from hooks attached to the wooden slats.

Stretching storage space is an ongoing challenge, met particularly well in these examples: Shelves, drawers, and cupboards are packed into a small corner unit (above). Minimal space beside an integrated-front built-in refrigerator-freezer (right) becomes an intimate snack-dining area, along with open shelves for display, glass-fronted cabinets to keep track of everyday items, and a closed cupboard where neatness doesn't count. A long under-cabinet shelf (opposite, top left) takes the curse off a too-shallow countertop. Unused space beside a fridge and under a wall cabinet (opposite, top right) becomes an open appliance garage. A standing knife rack (opposite, center right) pulls cutlery to safety out of drawers. One drawer is a pull-out cutting board. A "two-car" appliance garage (opposite, bottom right) can be made to disappear behind a single raise-up door.

GET CRAFTY When lack of counter space is an issue, a hideaway worktable could be a simple solution. This table could also serve as a makeshift breakfast site.

- Attach a board to the wall with hinges and paint it a glossy, easy-care finish that matches your wall color.

- Support the table from the wall with chains on hooks, so that when not in use, the table can be unhooked and folded down, out of the way.

SPICE PEARLS

DESIGN OPTIONS Because a kitchen is the center of life at home, it's essential that form and function mesh gracefully—certainly where storage is involved and specifically where spice storage is the focus. No matter which of the following ideas works for you, keep this motto in mind: Stay true to the way you cook, and make every inch count.

- In the prep zone, fit a pull-out drawer with sloping insert shelves so spice jars can be arranged in rows, tilted for easy access.

- If there is wall space beside your cooking appliance, install shallow shelves—either open or covered with a cupboard door—for spices.

- Shallow spice shelves hung on the back of cabinet doors in your meal-prep zone take little space but offer great convenience.

- Spice jars can be stored in an accessible way if arranged on a two-tier lazy Susan placed in an overhead cabinet, or arrayed on each shelf of a staircase-like storage unit designed to hold small containers.

- Make room in your prep zone for a small, narrow chest containing a set of apothecary drawers. These are scaled perfectly to the height of most spice jars. Such chests are best sought at local flea markets.

- Convert a skinny space between base cabinets into efficient spice storage. A custom pull-out unit, with two or even three shelves, can hold cooking oils and condiments as well as spices, and depending on where you put the unit, could be made accessible from two sides.

- You could also outfit an existing cabinet—a wall cabinet instead of a base cabinet—with an easy-to-install sliding shelf for spices.

- Spice racks can be hung where needed—either near your cooking appliances or the counters where you make your meals. These racks, which could be wood, plastic, or steel, can be moved as needed.

A butcher block–topped steel cart (top) can be rolled in or out of its base at the end of a kitchen island. Compactly designed, it has a shelf and storage drawers plus a steel rod where towels and tablecloths can be draped. In a chamfered corner (above), a two-tiered carousel is lit so nothing gets lost or overlooked. Drawers in two sizes and finishes are displayed here (right), to show the flexibility of drawer design and the way storage can be maximized, if well thought out, in a modest kitchen.

Clustered close to the built-in microwave plus drawer and cupboard storage (above) is a two-door pantry with open shelves that roll out at the touch of a finger so all of the contents are quickly visible. For collectors of antiques who hankered for an efficient 21st-century kitchen (above, right), a made-to-fit butcher block—topped worktable—it's new but looks old—provides a wide shelf and a shallow drawer as well as a very functional work surface. Elegant wall-hung wood shelves above it keep often-used products within arm's reach, and a steel shelf mounted against the range backsplash is wide enough to hold small cookware. Corner convenience is enhanced by a custom bow-front cabinet (right) designed to hold tableware as well as packaged goods, which gets ideal placement beside a built-in wall oven and microwave.

Storage abounds in kitchens designed for home entertaining (clockwise from top, left): The smallest drawer, carved into the mantel hiding the range hood, is apothecary size; a wide shelf, designed to display collectibles, tops the mantel; twisted rope columns add an Italianate accent to base cabinets; two rows of plate racks are centered above the sink, between storage niches; three open drawers pull out of one base cabinet, and a microwave disappears behind two swing-out doors when not being used.

Urban chic defines the airy kitchen in a house built in the woods (clockwise from above): The island's drawers, shelves, and cupboards fit together like pieces of a classic wood puzzle; a large open niche, set between wall ovens and the refrigerator, doubles as work and display space; niches in various shapes add breathing room and even more display space; the carefully divided utensil drawer makes every cubic inch count.

Check out these idea-filled storage stretchers (vertically, row by row): Airy wire vegetable drawers under a counter; dishtowels on a narrow pull-out rack; trays and baking tins in a standing rack. Utility items accessible in a two-level drawer unit; drawers sectioned off for utensils; home for spices in three pull-out drawers. Condiments arranged in a tall pull-out pantry; a mini-pantry in a cabinet built under a cooktop; spice shelves on the back of a cabinet door. Sponges in a tilt-out under-sink drawer; a cookware cabinet with a deep wire shelf affixed to a cabinet door; spice storage in a base-cabinet drawer. A tambour-door garage for small appliances; exposed dishtowels in an open niche; storage racks on wheels for flexibility. A drawer just for knives; roll-out spice shelves in a wall cabinet.

4 | KITCHEN EXTRAS

THE KITCHEN HAS NOT ONLY COME OF AGE. It has also matured in size and function. Where once it was a bland service—and often, servant's—zone, it has expanded its embrace to include a bartending center, various types of storage pantries—walk-in as well as built-in—and an ever-richer variety of places to eat. Often there is a breakfast room that flows seamlessly out of the kitchen proper, or a banquette at one end of the room beside a window with a patio and garden view. But in many kitchens there is just room enough for three or four stools to stand on one side of an island or peninsula, an area used not only for quick meals and breakfasts but also as a gathering spot for youngsters doing homework and guests making small talk. Yes, being the center of life in today's homes, the kitchen is where people entertain, or at least where hosting a dinner party usually begins and the family cook becomes the indisputable star.

An under-counter beverage center is paired with a wine cooler in a compact storage unit beyond the dining table in this large, open eat-in-kitchen (opposite). Platters, bowls, and glassware stand on open shelves; bar gear and serving utensils are kept in the drawer to the right of the appliance duo; unrefrigerated beverages are stored in the closed cupboard below that drawer.

KITCHEN DINING

Eat-in spaces are convenient and step-saving. You pull a dish out of the oven, the fridge, or the microwave, pivot without hardly moving your feet, and serve a meal instantaneously. Storage is rarely an issue, because dining and kitchen spaces are one. Along with two-sided islands and peninsulas—where people perched on stools become part of the action—the old-fashioned kitchen table has won new adherents who interpret this convenience in various ways.

DESIGNER SOLUTIONS Heather Moe, a Southern California–based kitchen designer, explains how she directs her clients in determining how much storage to include in the plan. In every instance, she is determined to create a place for everything that needs to be stored:

- "When I do a new kitchen for clients, I have them stand in the middle of their existing kitchen and ask them to put everything away."

One end of a beautiful paneled custom bench (below) pulls out, revealing a catchall storage drawer—for everything from seat cushions and tablecloths to kids' sports gear. This kitchen's dining corner faces a window and a glass door that leads out to a sun-kissed patio.

- "Next, I give them a pencil and ask them to write down everything they want to store in their kitchen. I get them to focus on one side first and make sure that every single thing that's in their kitchen has a place to be stored."

- "What this exercise almost always does is help us find something we didn't know about, whether it's a turkey platter or an oversize mixer."

- "It helps to also have elevation drawings—a plan isn't enough."

- "I also ask clients to add labels to the plan—to actually write 'place mats' or 'silverware' on their drawer fronts. By having them label their drawers and other storage areas, I can help them make sure, for example, that the drawers they plan to put their place mats in are wide enough."

- "My point here is to involve my clients in the process, to let them take on the responsibility of organizing things themselves, a job that's very hard to do at random without sitting in your actual kitchen."

PRACTICAL SUGGESTIONS

In arranging or rearranging storage elements in your kitchen, or planning new or remodeled kitchen space, think of how its spaces and amenities are likely to be used. Would a helpful guest know where, logically, to locate a spatula, frying pan, blender, mixing bowl, or serving tray?

- Map out a strategy to determine what items in the kitchen area must be readily available for most meals every day and which items could be stored elsewhere to make more room.

- If additional storage space is unavailable, think about where it might be created. One often-overlooked space is under the stairs—a staircase leading to upper floors or down to the basement. Open up one entire side below a staircase and you have a triangle measuring about three feet deep and seven or eight feet wide, which can be put to use for shelves or cabinets, either freestanding or built-in.

- No matter where in the kitchen you plan to dine, set up a storage system. Store items in the same place all the time, so you and whoever is helping you cook, serve, or just set the table won't have to spend time on a hunt for key items. It may be difficult, but the effort will pay off.

- Encourage members of your family to maintain whatever system you establish. You'll save time, of course, but also will be able to keep track of items that may need to be repaired or replaced.

Benches with a dual mission are built into the breakfast nook (above) of an expanded kitchen. A drawer beneath the built-in bench holds cushions and pillows; glasses and tall beverage bottles are stored neatly in the tall, narrow drawer that pulls out of the bench back.

CONVENIENCE AND VISIBILITY Today's home cooks seldom enjoy being isolated—shut off from family and friends while preparing a meal. That's one reason the open kitchen has such incredible appeal. There is a dark side to the issue, of course: Every item in the kitchen is visible, which means neatness is a prime objective, along with the perennial need to create a place for everything that must be stored. It's rare today for anyone to be able to close a door on a messed-up kitchen. Constant maintenance is a must—and a burden.

- Items stored on open shelves add interest to any kitchen space, even when family members or close friends are having a meal there. The secret lies in creating attractive arrangements—napkins in baskets, for example, plates in accessible racks or stacked by size, cups hung from hooks in neat rows, spices on trays or arranged in racks.

- If clutter is a concern, why not pretend you are a guest who has been asked to sit at the kitchen table or squat on a stool tucked under the island? From that vantage point, what do you see? If clutter and chaos are what crowd your vision, clearly there are too many items exposed or displayed. If everything is hidden behind closed doors—and the

Tall columns frame the opening between kitchen and dining area (below), and a long console adds storage as well as definition. Folded tablecloths and place mats are laid in the wide, shallow drawers; serving pieces are stored on the shelves.

Multicolored panes in a pantry door (above) create a geometric backdrop for a dining table set beside tall windows at the far end of an expanded kitchen. A round breakfast table (above, left) is at the center of an L-shaped kitchen whose owners enjoy the intimacy of dining a few steps from where they cook.

feeling of serenity verges on emptiness—perhaps some items can be brought out of hiding and placed where they will create visual interest.

- Although attractive and certainly convenient, any items put on display become vulnerable to accumulated dust and grime. One way to prevent this is to make sure that whatever is left out—stacked on open shelving or hung from hooks—is either used and replaced regularly or rotated so they will stay clean and not be dust-catchers.

- Except for the cookbooks you turn to often, most of your kitchen library probably could be stored in shelves on the dining side of your island or peninsula, or in storage niches cut into the ends of banquette benches. Books on open shelves should be pulled out and wiped on occasion.

- Home laundries and eat-in kitchens are not a good mix. If your kitchen plan involves a place to pause for breakfast or a quick snack, staring at even the handsomest washers and dryers is not a pleasure. Can the laundry area be tucked behind cabinet doors—either swing-out styles or bifolds? Or can you simply hang fabric, cut to size, to create an attractive distraction and a convenient shield?

ISLAND CAVEAT A kitchen island adds work space and storage, too, if there is room for shelves and cupboards. But the countertop can be a collection point for various types of clutter.

- Make sure that kids' games, magazines, newspapers, or incoming and outgoing mail do not stay long on the island countertop.

- Serenity is an essential. An island countertop must be cleared and ready for use in making or eating meals, any time of day.

A bench beneath the window (above) adds seating to a table positioned for informal dining, and also adds storage, in pull-out drawers underneath. A painted wooden table with a butcher-block top (right) extends outward from a cushioned banquette. Beside it, on the same wall, is a tall, narrow wine cooler (far right) and a drawer-fronted work surface that pulls out of a unit that stores glassware and bar essentials.

Leather-upholstered chairs pull up to a long wooden dining table (above) that faces a large pass-through to the kitchen. Surrounding this opening is a custom bar unit, with wine racks, glassware storage, drawers for table accessories, and two under-counter wine coolers. The countertop flanking a range (left) extends outward to form a notched-in surface that is either bonus work space or a gracious table for two.

PANTRY PASSIONS

THE TRADITIONAL STORAGE ROOM This was really a staple, not a luxury, in a great many homes as late as the early decades of the 20th century. Sometimes it was open space at the end of a kitchen; other times it was a separate room. But in every instance it had shelves for canned and packaged foods—sometimes fresh foods as well— and also for everyday glassware and tableware. What made the room convenient was that everything was out in the open—no need to launch a major search to ferret out an unopened jar of peanut butter or mayonnaise. With the arrival of the millennium, the traditional pantry didn't just disappear; it evolved. Often it remained a separate space, usually with a solid or glass door. It also became integrated into new-kitchen design, and with roll-out shelving included in many pantry designs, it became an even more convenient and accessible way to store.

A 36-inch-wide custom stainless steel cabinet (above) is recessed into transition space between a dining room and kitchen. Perforated steel panels soften the look but let people see what is stored on upper shelves. There is a surfeit of shelving in this windowed pantry (right), but the secret of its success is its organization. Glassware, storage jars, and condiments are clustered, so no one has to ponder where items are located.

PANTRY CUPBOARDS Pantries that are there when you need them and hidden when you don't are high on most homeowners' wish lists. Ideally, these are built-in units incorporated into a kitchen's total cabinet design, but if space exists—or can be uncovered—pantry functions can be relegated to freestanding cabinets.

- If you decide to include a pantry in your kitchen design or make room for one in an existing kitchen, make a list of what you plan to store there. The list will provide a clear indication of the number of shelves to create and also how tall each shelf should be.

- Be aware that standard pantry-shelf depth ranges between 18 and 24 inches. Deeper shelves will certainly hold more items but will also make accessibility to items way in the back problematic. That's why roll-out shelving has become so popular. Once the shelf rolls out, accessibility ceases to be an issue.

- If ventilation within a pantry is needed, consider baskets on open shelves or freestanding wire shelves and racks, which would be ideal for any fresh food products you plan to store.

- Consider the possibility of pantry doors. Yes, they conceal your goods, but they also have their own storage potential if you can mount shelves along the inside surfaces. A row of shallow shelves mounted on door interiors could be the perfect place to store spices and salad dressings. If there are youngsters in the household, lower door shelves could be accessible repositories for packaged snacks and cereals.

- Pull-out pantries are tops in convenience, because the entire unit pulls out of a cabinet wall, not just individual shelves. Some of these units fit into base cabinets; others rise from floor level to the top of the wall cabinets. And, of course, sometimes there is more than one pantry unit in a kitchen. Let space and need be the touchstones.

- Locating a built-in pantry definitely does involve space availability and cooking style. Some homeowners place their pull-out pantry beside their built-in refrigerator, or flank their refrigerator with tall, narrow units. It's also possible to place a pantry deeper into the food-prep zone—beside a work island or peninsula, or adjacent to a range or cooktop. What you plan to store there will also affect your choice.

- The perfect contemporary pantry may well be the narrow one that pulls out and is accessible from not one but both sides, which means that wherever you happen to be at work in the kitchen, stored goods can be spotted and reached in a heartbeat.

- Because of their convenience, and also because their contents are rarely visible to anyone other than the person who opens them, pantries can become dumping places, and thus should be inventoried often.

An oak counter unifies the bar area (above) with kitchen cabinetry. Here, drawers and cupboards hold all of a household's entertaining needs, and open shelving—tucked in a niche—lets gleaming glassware be displayed. Just beyond the kitchen, a refrigerator-freezer is integrated into custom cabinetry. Note the roller latches and strap hinges, which recall old-fashioned iceboxes.

A two-sided pantry with wire shelves for beverages, packaged cereals, and condiments (top) pulls out of a wall of cabinets that surround wall ovens. A fully equipped butler's pantry fills one end of a sharply contemporary kitchen (above). Glassware resides on open shelves and behind frosted-glass doors.

BUTLER'S PANTRIES Once considered a luxury—and a surefire component of a kitchen designed for hired pros—the butler's pantry has crept nobly into contemporary kitchen design and in many households is as much a staple as a work zone near the sink.

- Space and budget are the determinants here. If there is room for a separate zone for storing and serving refreshments—and if you choose to entertain often enough to justify this inclusion—a butler's pantry will neatly fit your kitchen needs.

- In a traditional household, the butler's pantry could be a separate adjunct, one shaped like a galley kitchen—with amenities on two sides. This type of butler's pantry could absorb, or be created as, a short corridor leading from kitchen to dining room.

- A super-luxurious butler's pantry would have its own separate bar sink plus a wine cooler and perhaps also a beverage center, so that whoever is serving drinks will never have to intrude on the traffic patterns of anyone working in the heart of the kitchen.

- Depending on how heavy your year-round entertaining load may be, under-counter appliances such as a separate wine cooler and soft-drink refrigerator may be superfluous, except for one: an ice maker. This would add an important dimension of convenience to the kitchen of any household where guests are likely to turn up.

- In many a home, the kitchen remains the domain of the hostess; the butler's pantry, that of the host. But tradition has been deconstructed, and often the host is the chef and the hostess tends bar. It hardly matters who is anointed to serve drinks to guests; what counts is where the butler's pantry is placed and how many items it can store.

- A reserve supply of soft drinks can be kept in butler's pantry cabinetry, and for high visibility, even in cabinets with glass-fronted doors. For safekeeping, hard liquor belongs in cabinets with solid doors and, as an extra precaution—particularly if there are young people in the household—behind lockable doors.

- Although you may want to display your wedding-gift crystal in a dining room breakfront, those tumblers and wine and martini glasses you call on for informal predinner refreshment could be kept on overhead cabinet or open shelves. The idea here is to keep such items separate from the milk, juice, and water glasses in use every day. This arrangement would constitute a basic butler's pantry, which could simply be an isolated corner of the kitchen.

- A butler's pantry is a logical place in which to keep a wine rack, depending on how vast your wine collection is. Red wines should be stored on their sides or in gently sloping slots. Such wine racks could be installed in closed cabinets or, if necessary, placed on a butler's pantry countertop.

■ It may be ideal to keep counter space free and open, but perhaps not always possible. Best advice: Stored red wines will live best at room temperature, so make sure wine racks are not placed near heating units or cooking appliances.

STORAGE FURNITURE

Kitchen cabinets are really pieces of furniture. Yes, many of them are built-in and exist in long runs, but even so, the style of their doors—the paneling, the trim—would place them in the category of furniture. In most homes, white melamine or laminate cabinets hark back to the past. Even the manufacturers of so-called stock (premeasured) cabinets include furniture-quality styling and often some details in the pieces they make.

FREESTANDING PIECES

The English kitchen designer Johnny Grey achieved a design breakthrough, some years ago, by promulgating the "unfitted kitchen." He conceived of kitchens comprising a series of individual-seeming pieces of furniture rather than cabinet runs. His ideas changed the way a great many kitchen cabinetmakers designed their products; they also gave people license to include furniture pieces in their kitchen plans.

■ If there is room, a hutch or breakfront could dominate one wall of a kitchen, for storing glassware or serving pieces. The only caveat here is to make sure the hutch's style complements that of the cabinets you select.

Adding a note of classic elegance to a remodeled kitchen is this giant hutch (below), which holds a vast collection of Depression-era glass on two tiers of glass-fronted cabinets. Closed cabinets hold trays, serving pieces, and barware.

Part of a lineup of custom cabinetry with a panel that fronts the fridge (top) is a hutch with shelves for display, drawers and cupboards for storage. An old unpainted pantry (above) fits in a corner; it sits on the counter but is also anchored to the wall. What looks like an eight-drawer chest (right) is actually a storage cabinet with shelves and a place where a food processor rises when needed and lowers when not in use.

- An armoire is another possibility, as it's a piece of furniture with drawers or cupboards and plenty of shelf space for storing linens, place mats, coasters, and cocktail napkins.

- Small chests could also be added to an extended kitchen plan. They might be useful in creating the semblance of a barrier between a kitchen and dining room, or kitchen and family room. And also, of course, they could be enlisted to hold flatware and serving utensils.

- Storage pieces you acquire at flea markets or auctions could also be useful, as long as you have scale in mind before you make a purchase. Know that you have room for them—carry your floor plan with you when you shop—and that they will have a positive purpose; otherwise, they will be cumbersome and, ultimately, superfluous.

- It's possible to give an old chest, cupboard, or cabinet a new life by refitting it with sturdy new shelves and hardware that coordinates with what exists or has been chosen for your kitchen cabinets.

- When thinking about adding individual storage units, look for possibly overlooked spots—an unused corner, awkward wall space between windows, anywhere built-ins might be inappropriate. As a homey philosopher once said, "There's a lid for every pot," which in this context means that if you love it, you can probably make it work.

- What might not work in any contemporary context is furniture that is truly antique. A hardy country piece might be durable, but some antique pieces have shaky doors and even shakier drawers—parts that would not withstand heavy daily use.

- Where you place an antique piece will be key to how you use it. Off in a corner, or as a transition piece from the kitchen to the hall or the rest of a great room, it might make a handsome decorative accent, a piece you use to store items you seek out very rarely. If you find it, love it, and have room for it somewhere, buy it or you may long regret not doing so. Just don't make it a kitchen workhorse.

- The scale of some antique pieces may be more in keeping with homes from the 19th and early 20th centuries. That's why scale is so important when you introduce a random freestanding piece.

- More practical, because of their flexibility, are low cupboards or chests that could be moved as needed, their surfaces useful when serving food or drinks, or as places to put plants or bowls of flowers when adding color or touches of nature is called for.

A pantry pulls out of a tall, narrow cabinet (above) just beyond the kitchen's second sink and harlequin-patterned mosaic backsplash. This space-saving, ceiling-high unit is designed to hold a family's entire supply of packaged foods.

A pantry cabinet with shelves built into the inside panels of both of its doors (above) has open shelves for much-sought items and deep drawers structured to hold heavy equipment. The cupboard above is ideal for items not in frequent use. Frosted glass partly obscures the contents of pantry shelves that hold a family's colorful everyday dishes (above, right). This section of a larger unit, twice the size of what is shown here, is set into the kitchen's far wall, convenient to the undermount sink, drawer dishwasher, and (not shown) the separate freestanding refrigerator and freezer. A wooden shelf unit (right) revolves at the touch of a fingertip to make every item in this custom pantry easy to find and access. Six shelves in each of the two doors make room for various often-used items to be seen and quickly retrieved.

KITCHEN DECOR Purists often deride the idea of decorating a kitchen, considering this a functional space that should not be compromised by any decorating touches. But consider how much use today's kitchens get. Why shouldn't whatever touches or accents that make living rooms inviting and homey also be found in kitchens?

- Consider color your most creative decorating tool. Even if you opt for plain white cabinets, you could back them with walls painted in rich, warm colors or with wall coverings in compelling patterns.

- Without cluttering the space, you could display a sampling of items you collect, whether these are old pitchers or small vintage spoons.

- Add simple charm to any kitchen with even a small wall display of old or antique utensils—well-worn objects that bespeak an earlier time.

An integrated pull-out pantry (above) is accessible from two sides. Its steel wire shelves hold bottled and packaged products in handy reserve, close to both the kitchen on one side and the dining room on the other. Coordinated hardware makes the three-door refrigerator and two-door pantry (left) appear a matched pair. Narrow niches stacked between the two units provide floor-to-ceiling wine storage.

Everything in one place: Tall doors made of translucent glass set into aluminum frames (left) cover multiple shelves within a built-in storage wall whose capacity rivals that of what once would have been a separate pantry room.

Mostly visible kitchen storage is confined to a pair of tall shelves that flank the refrigerator-freezer (opposite, near right) and double shelves with hinged gull-wing doors that fold upward, hung to the left of the cooktop and oven. A complete set of recycling bins (top, right) is mounted within drawers that pull out beneath a stainless steel kitchen sink. Part of a hanging storage system, these shallow steel shelves (opposite, far right) were designed to hold sets of glassware and ceramic containers.

5 | WORK-SPACE INNOVATIONS

TODAY'S HOME OFFICE IS WHEREVER YOU ARE. For many people, fast-growing technology has reduced office needs to a lightweight laptop and portable digital gear that can provide instantaneous links to every corner of the world. Still, it's always good to have a home base, a place where papers can be spread out, where financial and business records can be kept, and often where visiting partners or clients can relax and talk business. Devoting an entire room to home-office functions continues to be a luxury, particularly if it's an office with its own door. So, for most people who do business at home, an office may be the corner of a bedroom or family room, or an extension of the kitchen. Or It could be a room that also serves as a guest room. Whether it occupies a long wall, just a niche, or a separate room with a door, a home office is a perennially important component of home design, remodeling, and space planning, as the ideas that follow suggest.

A custom office wall (above), with drawers for records, and cupboards and shelves for supplies, is an ideal solution for someone working at home. Different tastes and differing needs dictated the design of what is actually a two-person home office (opposite). The built-in desks are close together but positioned so nobody feels crowded.

PRACTICAL APPROACHES It's no trick to keep whatever space is set aside for a home office neat and organized; what may be tricky, and often challenging, is controlling the inevitable clutter. Piles of documents and a profusion of sticky notes may be great reminders of what's next on the to-do list, but spread out all over your desk or any other flat surface, or even parts of the floor, they can become unsightly. File, recycle, or shred no-longer-needed papers and disposable mail every day. And when planning or expanding home-office space, be sure you have enough room for whatever must be stored.

- Measure your needs, just as you would in planning a kitchen or redoing a closet. Is there enough cupboard and drawer space to hold your work as well as essential backup supplies?

- Before buying or bringing in any new storage, empty existing drawers, clear off surfaces, and wipe everything down. Sort what you've saved: papers to file, supplies, gadgets, and tools. Separate out all the items you need to have at your fingertips, such as your calendar, address book, or whatever personal digital assistant you have been using.

- Designate drawers, bins, or boxes for everything. Labels can help you put items back where you've decided they belong. Drawers and desktop accessories will be useful in keeping small items accessible.

Desktop accessories can be utilitarian without looking pedestrian. Glass and ceramic pieces (below) easily make clip and pencil storage look glamorous. Two file drawers topped with a laminate-covered wooden slab (below, right) comprise a desk on a balcony overlooking a two-story living room. A high-back adjustable desk chair and built-in daybed complete this picture of superior home-office comfort.

- Take time to talk to your financial adviser or accountant and find out how long you need to keep certain documents and tax records.

LOCATION, LOCATION, LOCATION It hardly matters where you establish a home-office setup. The key to its success will be how you use whatever space you designate—for doing work and also for storing whatever you want to keep.

- It's the rare household that has more than enough storage space, and home offices tend to be the areas that get short shrift. Thus, creative storage is critical. Think of places to tuck built-in cubbies, cabinets, shelving, and desks by appropriating space from a hallway, an alcove, or an area adjacent to a bedroom closet.

Floor to ceiling, wall to wall, a home office in one corner of the kitchen (above, left) is both out of the way and close to the action. The French-country desk (above) placed between family-room windows is just a decorative element when closed. But when opened and paired with a white-painted chair, it becomes a useful spot for making notes, paying bills, and even writing letters.

Sunlight beaming through clerestory windows (below) helps brighten an eat-in kitchen whose recessed home office is set between an integrated-front refrigerator and an outside door. A built-in desk plus shelving for supplies (below, right) is set into a kitchen's far corner, just beyond the peninsula. Cabinet style and finish are consistent with overall kitchen design, as is the tile backsplash. A bar-height desk (opposite) was added to the end of a run of cabinets that provide storage above as well as beside the refrigerator-freezer. The stool can be moved to the breakfast bar, if needed.

- Unless your home office is in a distant corner, it's likely to be used at various times by more than one family member. Make sure there are labeled storage facilities—baskets, plastic containers, or shelves—so that optimal order can be maintained and confusion is minimal.

- Even if no actual business is ever done at home, an office of sorts is a modern-day essential. Every household needs a place where mail is processed, bills are paid, and records are kept. If this place happens to be the kitchen, the home office is also where recipes are stored and studied. How the space will be used, and by whom, will determine where, ideally, a home office should be located.

- In a household with children running in, out, and around, a home office will be beset with sound and movement. So it's not surprising that people seek out remote places to establish an office beachhead.

A finished basement is a possibility. Overhead noises could become a discouraging distraction, however.

- Don't plant an office in the middle of the basement; just section off a corner. Even so, you may have more room than you need, which could be an advantage. With good overhead lighting, you should be able to compensate somewhat for the lack of sunshine.

Home offices tucked into kitchens are not unusual; what makes these examples special is how little space they absorb and how much storage they include. A cluttered bulletin board over a four-drawer desk (above) creates a lively contrast to a display of collectibles in lighted overhead cabinets. Looking like an appendage to a built-in refrigerator-freezer, this 30-inch-wide desk (right), adjacent to shelves for cookbooks, pictures, and objects—even a tiny lamp—is the perfect spot for serious recipe study and meal planning.

- Is there raw attic space that could be converted into an office? If so, it will need a finished wall and floor, in addition to heating and cooling appliances. Access, too, might be challenging; many an old-house attic is reachable only by narrow and rather forbidding fold-down stairs or an ancient, unsteady ladder. But having home and office under the same roof could be appealing enough to justify the inconvenience.

- What about modifying a generous-size prebuilt tool or garden shed, a structure with designed-in, packaged weather protection? It could be placed far enough away from the house for privacy but close enough for convenience.

- Few homes have a truly spare closet, but for some homeowners, the idea of replacing closet shelves, hooks, and rods with a built-in desk and storage units would be a favorable solution. One major plus: There's already a door to shut when the office is not being used.

A backless stool can be pushed out of the way if action at the sink end of this kitchen (above) gets busy. This is mainly a place for bill paying, but it's wired so that a cordless phone can be recharged and a laptop can be used to send and receive e-mails. A pull-down message center (left) is one component of figured-ash custom cabinetry beyond a kitchen peninsula. There is a shelf for a venerable TV; it is installed and displayed above a computer, which is exposed and usable when a tall drawer front folds down flat to become a desk.

MULTIPURPOSE MATTERS If your home office ends up being space shared with other users with dissimilar purposes, there are things to do to dress it up so that office functions do not appear to dominate.

- Bring in a daybed and a scattering of throw pillows. You'll have extra seating by day and a sleeping amenity for guests by night. Look for the daybeds that have slide-out storage underneath—a welcome bonus.

- Move in a floor lamp with an adjustable arm, either for additional targeted task lighting or ambient illumination.

- Enlist a cubbyhole-style shelf unit to serve various functions. Arrange books (always by subject matter) for easy reference on one level and place color-coordinated magazine files on another.

- Create and implement a consistent labeling system, whether your shared office has closed cupboards or open storage. Small tags on baskets or wicker bins are attractive ways to organize and store videos, discs, and any other items you want to keep within arm's reach. Even if what you store is fully exposed, when arranged or stacked neatly it will be unobtrusive—less likely to acquire the taint of clutter.

- Incorporate decorative objects sparingly into open shelves and cubbies; displaying just a few much-loved pieces will have greater impact than letting it all hang out.

GET CRAFTY Depending on where you need to place a desk, you can improvise one by turning a flat, stained, or painted door on its side and supporting it with a two- or three-drawer file cabinet at each end. Or you can actually build a desk into a chosen spot.

- Calculate the height, width, and depth of the space. Measure in three places since walls are not always even.

- Plan the placement of the desktop (30-inch height is standard for adult use) and accompanying shelves. Using a carpenter's level as a guide, mark with masking tape where everything will go.

- Have shelves cut to size—either by a local lumber dealer or carpentry shop or on a circular saw in your own garage or basement—and set them on precut brackets, available at lumberyards and home centers.

- For desktop supports, measure the length and width of the work surface and cut six 1-by-2-inch pine boards—two lengths, and four pieces each 2 inches shorter than the width. Secure one long board flat against the back wall and two short pieces against the side walls at the wall studs. Attach each remaining board perpendicularly to its counterpart, creating an upside-down "L." Lay the desk surface on top; use nails or flat-head screws to fasten it to the supports.

DESK JOBS Whether you buy it, build it, or improvise very cleverly, plan to tailor your desk to the room's scale. Note that you will need a surface at least 30 inches deep for a desktop computer. Desk width will depend on the type and volume of work you have to do.

- Curb visual clutter by hanging a serene painting over the desk rather than a busy bulletin board (which may be less of a distraction if mounted on an adjacent wall). Add blinds or decorative window shades to limit outside distractions.

- When furnishing, include a decorative table lamp with an adjustable three-way bulb. That way it can shed strong task light during office hours and supply softer illumination when workday chores are over.

- An attractive lighting alternative is a wall-mounted swing-arm lamp that can be manipulated to provide task light where needed and then be swung back, out of the way, when not.

Stock units from a versatile cabinet manufacturer were assembled to create a desk (above) that occupies its own corner at the edge of a kitchen. The central overhead cabinet holds office supplies; the cupboards are fitted out for hanging files. Space and comfort define a sofa-equipped home office (opposite), located right outside a kitchen but continuing that room's clean-lined contemporary aesthetic. Color and pattern brighten the office, whose spare look can be attributed to substantial storage space. Books are exposed; so is the computer keyboard. But all other office essentials are cannily concealed.

6 | INTIMATE EXCELLENCE

ROOMS THAT FAMILY MEMBERS RETREAT TO deserve as much storage consideration as the front hall or the formal dining room, spaces that guests see and experience. Kids often complain about how pointless it is to keep their bedrooms tidy because nobody else but themselves and a few friends ever see the clutter. The truth is that an uncluttered space is the most livable one. Whether it's a couple sharing bedroom, bathroom, and closet spaces or children trying to organize clothing, book, and toy storage, all would be measurably ahead of the game in well-organized rooms with adequate, well-thought-out storage. Whether you have elbow room to spare or make do in cramped quarters, the quest for suitable storage is limitless. And it is certainly true that the more space you have, the more you'll use. Note that designers are not the only experts to solve the space puzzle; a great many homeowners are also recognizably brilliant innovators.

A play area–sleeping loft stacked atop an open closet (opposite) was a solution for a creative family eager to be innovative on behalf of their child. The clothing rack is mounted low enough so the youngster can reach it. A ceiling-skirting open shelf is for books and toy soldiers, equally accessible when the youngster climbs a ladder his dad made for him.

An oversize dresser (above) dominates one wall of a compact guest bedroom. This custom unit is tall—to reach top drawers, a stool is pulled the closet— but storage space is shallow, so nothing impedes the flow of sunlight. A fold-down Murphy bed (below) makes a guest room out of an alcove. Wall-wide top cabinets hold blankets and pillows.

BEDROOM CHALLENGES

Whether the space is reserved for visiting friends and relatives, is the exclusive preserve of two spouses, or is a work-play-sleep zone for a passel of children, bedroom storage is ultimately a primary concern. Whomever they are intended for, a home's bedrooms have one thing in common: At some point in the day they become retreats, the places where people wind down, withdraw from the rest of the household, and rest or sleep. Bedroom decorating is usually geared toward soft colors, soothing comfort, and an unthreatening mood. Clutter is a predictable no-no, which is why storage considerations here are essential.

MOOD CONTROL "As your bedroom is where you start and end your day," says cable-TV host and design authority Christopher Lowell, "it should be a place where you feel pampered and completely at ease." He also insists that "clutter in a bedroom robs your sense of well-being more than anything else." His solution, one that he eagerly shares, is to display only what is attractive and visually interesting and keep everything else nicely hidden.

- One or more dressers with deep drawers should hold most clothing and accessory needs, but not every bedroom has space enough for massive pieces of furniture. An alternative might be shelf units placed judiciously, with elegant covered baskets that hold drawer contents. To avoid confusion, print out and attach discreet standard-size labels.

- Although not a new idea, a built-in headboard with shelving or cupboards on either side and open shelves overhead is always effective. Such a custom unit could solve a great many problems—book and gadget storage, and of course a way to put a number of favorite collectibles on display.

- Avoid crowding, thus cluttering, every flat surface. Keep in mind that displaying a handful of cherished treasures will garner more sincere attention than a tabletop jammed with miscellaneous objects.

- Hanging wall art—no garish colors or violent imagery—is appropriate here, but don't overdo. When in doubt, opt for a low-key look.

FURNITURE CHOICES Beyond the all-purpose dresser, there are other pieces to consider in furnishing a bedroom and accommodating a variety of storage needs. Keep in mind that flexibility, along with capacity, is a commendable goal. You want furniture that will continue to be serviceable in the years ahead, whether you remain in your home long-term or move many times in the near or distant future.

- Nightstands are the most common items of bedroom furniture beyond the beds themselves. If storage is a serious concern here, choose cabinets with shelves or drawers, or some of each. Having functional nightstands at bedside can solve a variety of storage needs.

- Books are logical bedroom accoutrements, and unless they are scattered throughout or placed in cumbersome stacks, they also provide legitimate visual interest. Today's furniture retailers sell bookcases in an array of heights and widths, which means that almost any spare wall or corner could be designated a spot for book storage.

- Depending on room size, the foot of a bed could be as useful for storage as the headboard. A low shelf unit—for books, baskets, or closed containers—would provide a surfeit of bed-width storage.

- An old or antique blanket chest or steamer trunk could also be placed at the foot of the bed. Either would be excellent repositories of bed linens, blankets, or anything else you want to stow but not show.

- If there is space under a bedroom window, how about building a window seat with one or more storage drawers underneath?

Family treasures are displayed nearly everywhere in a crowded but cozy master bedroom (above). They are seen on a side table, on top of an antique chest, and on one shelf of a ceiling-high hutch that holds towels and linens. What makes the room airy and inviting is transparent window treatments and the overall use of one color: white.

Serenity in the bedroom doesn't have to mean sterility. This is a personal retreat, after all, no matter whose bedroom it is, and here, certainly, an individual stamp is called for and expected. Entering the room should be a reminder that "this is *my* space." Collectibles and personal possessions—family photos or interesting pieces—deserve to be shown off. The secret, though, is to make each piece seem truly important.

- You don't have to display every handmade bowl or pitcher you own; make a point of rotating your collection. Why not make changes every few months and freshen the spaces you like to decorate? You'll find it joyful to rediscover something that's been tucked away unseen for a while and, at the same time, will also enjoy retiring items that have been on display a long time.

- Never fill every open storage shelf completely, from one end to the other. Leave open spaces, and on bookshelves remember to fill in with collectibles to enrich the display. Keep in mind: Less is more!

Closet space was spare in this minimal master bedroom (above), so the homeowner augmented her storage with a wall unit whose top shelf is for display items and whose wooden pegs hold clothing. Wall-mounted flea market finds (opposite)—shutters and frames in all sizes—are not only decorative but also places to display costume jewelry.

ROOMS FOR KIDS

Although it is generally accepted that youngsters should have a say in the way their personal spaces are furnished, it does remain the parents' responsibility to choose or suggest the best way to store the kids' possessions. Think of bedrooms for young people as homes within a home. In most instances, children will sleep, play, and entertain here. Sensibly planned storage will help make these multiuse spaces function.

- Whether redoing an existing space or creating a new one, draw up a plan on paper. That's the best way to ensure that whatever you build or buy will fit properly and keep the youngsters reasonably content.

Nearly grown up, the inhabitant of this bedroom (above) keeps walls mostly pure and hides most of her possessions in one bedside chest. Color and shape bring zest to a younger child's bedroom (below), with storage spots for toys and bulletin boards for displaying artwork.

- Before finalizing a room plan, get out a tape measure. You should estimate as accurately as possible how much storage space the room will actually need. This knowledge will be important if you are buying storage units; it will be even more important if you are having storage built in.

- As you plan, decide how best to organize the room. Consider creating areas or zones—one for sleeping, one for playing, one for doing homework, one for crafts. Your plan will reflect the child's interests, of course, and if the room is to be shared, the challenge will be greater.

- Children grow, and their needs will change. When laying out spaces in a young person's bedroom, keep the flexibility concept in clear focus. You may want to add pieces in the years ahead, and perhaps remove some pieces that no longer have a purpose. What you don't want to have to do—ever—is refurnish from scratch.

- Shelf units are always a good bet and a logical investment. Books can be stored there—games, too, as long as they are stacked neatly and arranged so labeling can be seen.

- A small chest with a raise-up lid is another possible inclusion—a great way to store toys and games. Put it on wheels for maximum mobility.

TOY PLOYS If there are young children in your home, you probably have literally stumbled on one or more of their toys in practically every room in the house. Reprimands may be in order after each occurrence, but they are unlikely to solve the problem.

- Work out toy storage plans with the kids themselves. If they help make the storage decisions, they may be more likely to abide by them.

- Closed cabinets may add to visible neatness but may also foment indescribable interior chaos—toys flung willy-nilly into cupboards without any thought given to where the best and most convenient storage spaces are.

- Bins—either solid or translucent plastic—will keep items at least partly visible, thus accessible, particularly if they are sized to the height and depth of the shelves they rest on. If youngsters know where to find a particular toy, they might respond more readily to putting that toy back whenever playtime ends.

- Create attractive labels—with either words or images—and apply them to storage containers. You might even color-code them: red for toys, green for games, blue for puzzles. If there is no doubt where an item lives, you can reasonably expect it to be kept there always.

In two more views of the child's room shown on page 88, a wall of cubbies (above) is a powerful aid to keeping a youngster organized. Recycled wood was used to build a four-inch platform for the youngster's bed (below), which just fits the upper area of a former closet.

- Reserve one or more areas for display—of photos of the children and their friends, of crafts items they have made, of trophies they have won or earned, and of any items of value they have collected. Let children add their own personalities to the spaces they inhabit.

THE CLOSET CHALLENGE

DESIGN ADVICE Closet organizing has become a lucrative facet of home design and a source of revenue for a number of firms that have outlets in various parts of the country. For a fee (one that is usually applied to any order you place), a design expert will visit your home, study your closet space, and listen to your needs, then send you a plan you can approve, thereby giving the nod to custom closet interior construction. It's possible, of course, for you to create an equally efficient facility on your own, without making a substantial investment.

- Start with one closet, maybe the worst one; do not attempt to work on more than one at a time.

- Take everything out, separating items into piles or areas denoting "Toss," "Give away," and "Keep." The idea here is to shave your inventory and store only those items that you will actually use or wear.

- Once you know exactly what must fit in the closet, you will also begin to know how much room you will need to store suits, jackets, skirts, robes, shoes, handbags, belts, and every other item that is likely to land in a closet, sometimes on the floor.

- If it's a shared closet, some kind of division will be needed—so that siblings and spouses alike know where their belongings go.

What was once wasted space outside a master bedroom (below) is now a man's dressing room–closet, with hanging rods, open shelves, and a made-to-measure chest—all in one unit. This floor-to-ceiling custom configuration eliminates the need for a bureau that would have created a cluttered look and squeezed the bedroom's limited space.

EFFICIENT SPACE-SAVERS Tidiness in a closet is more important than in almost any other area of home storage. Space is usually limited, and storage needs can be endless. Whether it's a closet for off-season gear, children's clothes, or his-and-hers adult wardrobes, a closet must present a convenient and also highly accessible arrangement, with often-needed items right up front and less frequently used or worn items stored somewhat out of reach but never totally out of sight. Keep in mind that you can fit much more into an organized closet than a cluttered one.

- Reserve high shelves for seldom-used items, like special-occasion accessories or out-of-season clothing. If the topmost shelf is more than 75 inches off the floor, plan on including a folding step stool in your closet furnishings.

- Note that folded clothing can get messy quickly, so keep casual pieces in bins or baskets that you can slide off a shelf, or stow them in stackable containers. Unless these are see-through containers, take time to label each one, so you don't have to guess or draw on occult powers when you're rushing to get dressed.

- Divide and conquer. To make optimal use of open shelving, seek out shelf dividers at a hardware store or home center. Such units clamp to the bottom of each shelf and can be spaced to provide only as much width as you indicate in order to store stacks of sweaters in a clothes closet or towels in a linen closet.

- Provide an equal amount of shelf help by attaching decorative brackets to the top of closet shelves rather than under them. Place them securely so they divide shelves into sections earmarked for sweaters, purses, and scarves that deserve to be stored in an organized way.

- If a closet is sizable enough, consider bringing freestanding storage furniture into it. For example, you can free up space in a bedroom by setting aside room for a chest or bureau in the closet. Since the unit will not be out in public view, it need only be efficient—and sturdy—not necessarily stylish. Demanding homeowners insist on painting or staining unfinished furniture for closet use.

- Don't overlook the inside surfaces of hinged closet doors. These are ideal and super-convenient spots for belt, robe, and handbag hooks, and for hanging shoe racks as well. Although there is usually adequate space between the door interior and whatever is stored within, make sure door storage is shallow. Restrict its use to absolute essentials.

- Exploit every inch of vertical space. If a folding step stool is kept handy, nothing that's stored should be difficult to reach or get at quickly.

In redesigning a master bath without stretching its existing footprint, the architect expanded the toilet area to include a needed linen closet (above). The angled space is not deep, but the storage shelves are adequate to hold all of the family's towel and linen needs.

CLOSET VARIATIONS Differing types of home storage facilities fall into the category of closets, nearly all of which have doors that close to contain the contents and hide the mess. The messiness factor tends to complicate home life, because it makes finding and retrieving stored items much more difficult. Best advice would be to keep every closet as neat as possible, as if the door were always open and everything inside illuminated by a bright spotlight.

■ Keep the guest closet near your front door in a state of welcoming neatness. If you use overhead shelves for off-season storage, make sure the items reside in labeled containers. And if you hang some of the family's winter outerwear on the rod, zip it up in clothing bags when the cold season ends. Most important, provide empty hangers (preferably wood, instead of wire) on a rod that has plenty of guest room.

■ Guest room closets are another potential clutter zone, as it is so easy to stack cartons on the floor or on sagging overhead shelves, and also to hang superfluous clothing on what may be a fairly short rod. Anything is possible, of course, in these admittedly spare storage zones, as long as neatness prevails and the clothes rod is kept spare for guest arrivals and also stocked with empty hangers.

■ Even if your guest room has a closet, or one exists nearby, the room itself should be furnished with a bureau or chest. You can fill a bottom drawer with household overflow, but be sure to welcome your guests with empty drawers so they can unpack without feeling intrusive.

■ Utility closets are the favored repositories for sports equipment, off-season outerwear, and sometimes luggage. Usually such closets are located far from public view, but that is no license for disorder. Cartons of boots or softball gear should be labeled clearly, so family members know where their stuff is stashed. If young children use a utility closet, their storage should be accessible on low-level shelving.

CLOSET SURROGATES If closet space is truly scarce, consider freestanding furniture to expand storage capacity. Such pieces often hold a lot and can add decorating flair wherever they are placed.

■ Armoires are a much-used closet substitute. They can add storage space to bedrooms, family rooms, entry halls, and even

Stylish curtains hide the contents of a narrow closet (top) whose rods, shelves, and shoe racks were easily assembled components from a home center. Zoned storage (above)—top, bottom, and to the side—enabled the homeowner to organize her possessions for easy accessibility. With drawer organizers (right), a lot can be stored in little space.

halls and kitchens. Depending on where you place such a piece, you can decide whether the cupboards or shelves are suitable for whatever you need to store. Sometimes armoires are utilized to expand clothes-closet capacity; equally often they are actually placed in closets to provide a seemingly built-in organizing system. Armoires go anywhere.

- Linen closets should be easy to keep neat. If sheets, pillowcases, towels, and washcloths are folded and stacked, fresh linens should always be evident and easy to reach. In a house that lacks a proper linen closet or where that closet is needed for another use, an armoire might be the answer. It can stand in the hall near bedrooms and baths, or it can be positioned against a wall within the bathroom. Wherever you put it, you will find that the armoire is a veritable storage workhorse.

OTHER OPTIONS Some work-at-home couples have converted big walk-in closets to office space; others have turned them totally into office-supply repositories. In each instance, organization is essential.

- Vary shelf height and depth to create individual zones; customize the space with storage gear that provides a uniform look. Label everything.

- Leave no inch unused. Up top, keep old tax returns; at mid-level, keep paper supplies. And make sure lighting throughout is adequate.

For a bedroom with insufficient closet space, three unpainted armoires were placed side by side on a wall between doorways (below). After applying coats of white paint, the homeowner added chunky hardware and affixed a black-and-white patterned wallpaper to the front of each door panel. The result is storage galore in a decorative setting.

LIBRARY LORE

TOO MANY BOOKS? People complain frequently that their homes are being overwhelmed by books, that their family rooms are taking on the stuffy, closed-in feeling of old school libraries. The problem is not so much that books exist in most households but that these books are not often stored appropriately.

- The best way to store books is by subdividing them: Separate them into categories and shelve them near where they are likely to be used.

- Every kitchen should have a cookbook library—a stack of shelves that contain cookbooks in current use. If space is tight, such books could be stowed just outside the kitchen—on laundry-room shelving, for example, or even on the upper shelves of a broom closet.

- You can have built-in shelving installed wherever you need it, but keep in mind that stock bookcases in a dizzying number of sizes are available at big-box stores and also at retail outlets where unfinished furniture is sold. An unfinished piece can be stained or painted to blend in with the color and style of whatever site you choose when placing it.

- Distribute book storage to the most suitable areas: light reading or the latest bestsellers in nightstands or on small shelf units in a bedroom; reference books and how-to manuals in the family room. Books of personal interest that have been read but need to be kept can be displayed in public places—in the living room or entry hall.

- Work with youngsters to help them organize their bookshelves; it's a way of underscoring a need to be respectful of every kind of book.

A lounging loft (above) was designed for balcony space above the great room in a mountain-view home in Colorado. A ladder reaches upper shelves; the sliding door shuts off the master bedroom. Shelving sufficient for storing a houseful of books (opposite) was built into one wall adjacent to a tall bedroom window, its dazzling shade fashioned from an embroidered bed cover from Uzbekistan.

In a modest home remodel, owners turned an undefined, unused area at the top of the stairs, just outside their bedroom, into an intimate library (above and opposite). They brought in bookcases and a comfortable armchair and ottoman, and chose gauzy curtains to make sure their decorative window treatment would not cut out the sun.

■ It was once considered fashionable to create a chair-high stack of books to place beside an armchair. Although that arrangement looked good in magazine photos, in reality it would be hazardous: Knocked over, it could damage the books as well as anything else in its path.

■ Think of books as decorating elements: They present interesting shapes and, with their jackets on, also present an incredible array of colors. Books enrich rather than overwhelm wherever you put them.

BOOK-STORAGE CAVEATS Stacked properly, books rarely require special care, but there are some significant storage no-nos:

■ Even if packed in cartons, books will dry out and become unstable if stored in an attic where temperatures fluctuate from hot to cold.

■ Similarly, the garage is no place for library overflow. Extreme temperatures can shorten book life. Thus, it would be better to donate excess books to a local library or charity than risk having them rot, over time.

■ Basement storage is dicey, unless yours is a finished basement. If you must store books in a raw basement, make sure the sealed cartons rest on wood planks raised a few inches above the concrete floor and pulled out a few inches from the wall. Dampness is books' enemy.

7 | BATHROOM BONUSES

TOILETS WERE ONCE TABOO. They were never shown, rarely written about, and talked about publicly mainly in whispers. Bathrooms themselves were called "necessary" spaces or rooms referred to mostly with euphemisms. Today, bathrooms have taken the spotlight. There are bathroom–dressing rooms, bathroom–fitness centers, and, of course, bathroom-spas fitted with fireplaces, digital TVs, and music systems.

Through this glamorous evolution, one staple has never changed: the need to store whatever must be kept in the bath. Which means bathrooms are always magnets for clutter. That ever-growing volume of jars and tubes, soaps and shampoos, sundries and medications, plus hair dryers and toilet tissue reserves can easily overwhelm a space. Where storage is concerned, baths are not unique. As with other spaces, the key to their ability to function well is good interior organization, along with watchdog maintenance.

L-shaped custom cabinetry turns part of a master bath (opposite) into a dressing room. The interlocked storage units are attached to the wall but raised above the floor, creating a less-than-bulky floating feeling. Translucent paper applied to the tall cabinet's glass panels is reflective, spreading light from flush ceiling fixtures throughout the room.

BATHROOM BASICS

Since the bath is no longer that room no one talks about, current and potential homeowners are frank in discussing family bath needs with their builders, designers, and architects. And—not surprisingly—every bath does have unique functions: Master baths are designed for a duo; children's baths, like those created for disabled persons, have accessibility features; guest baths, like powder rooms, are made to be inviting. All require places to store essentials conveniently.

IDEAL DESIGNS There is no single ideal bath, as every household and every bath-user has singular needs. The best bath is the one that works beautifully for whoever regularly uses it. Similarly, there is no single perfect bath location. Yes, the master bath should be adjacent, or as close as possible, to the master bedroom; the kids' bath should not be a long trek down two flights of stairs from their rooms; a powder room should be near a home's public areas. But it is also possible to put a bath in an attic or basement. Space remains the most significant luxury, for not only is sink and toilet clearance a concern, but so is the need to keep a whole catalog of bath supplies within arm's reach.

- In remodeling a bath, it's economical to install new fixtures where the old ones stood. But it is sometimes possible to increase bath-storage potential—not by disturbing the plumbing but by absorbing some or all of an adjacent closet or taking a nip out of an adjoining hall. Even if you can add only a few inches, that might be enough to create a niche for shelving or a cabinet that will hold towels or supplies.

- Pedestal sinks, which can bring individual shape and style to a bath, are not recommended in baths where storage is in short supply.

- Vanities, with their mix of drawers and cupboards, can be great space-savers, if cabinet interiors are organized and monitored regularly.

- Open-shelf units are a viable alternative for all but the most intimate bathroom supplies including, of course, any kind of medication.

- Especially in master baths, with dual-use vanities that may extend the width of the room, a sweep of closed cabinets could seem quite formidable. Open shelves relieve the mass. So do cabinets with either frosted- or ribbed-glass door fronts.

- Another way to interrupt the run of cabinetry comprising a long double vanity is by including a cabinet tower—a tall unit, with several drawers and perhaps a built-in laundry hamper—that subtly signals a division between the vanity's his-and-hers zones.

MULTIPLYING MEDICINE CABINETS Traditionally, there was only one, usually placed directly over the bathroom's single sink. Then, when dual sinks gained popularity, so did dual medicine cabinets. Gradually, they gained in size and capacity, sometimes with inside-door shelving and sometimes, too, with lockable compartments in which to store potent or dangerous drugs.

- Its mirrored-door front enables a medicine cabinet to reflect more light, natural or artificial. Cabinet depth tends to be standard. Height can vary, though; the taller the cabinet, the greater its storage capacity.

- In seeking ways to add storage to even a modest-size bathroom, don't overlook the possibility of adding another medicine cabinet. It need not be cut into the wall; it can just hang free. And as it probably would not be installed right over a sink, it could hold seasonal medications—such as suntan lotions, burn emollients, and winter cold remedies.

- Note that a medicine cabinet doesn't have to look like one. It could be a small-scale vintage cupboard hung on the wall or standing on a counter. It could also be a narrow chest with shallow drawers—proof that horizontal storage can be just as efficient as vertical. Whenever limited space is an issue, compromise makes sense.

- Unfortunately, medicine cabinets are very often the places where powerful medications in half-empty bottles stand indefinitely. If you were to query a physician, he would certainly advise tossing drugs that have been around for more than a year, and urge never reusing a drug without a fresh prescription even if you think the illness you have now is just like the one the drug was originally prescribed to heal. Some doctors are likely to urge that old drugs be flushed away, rather than simply tossed.

Two tall cabinets, with cupboards and drawers, flank a pedestal sink (above). In remodeling, the homeowner ripped out the bathroom vanity, preferring individual units to a built-in's bulk. In a large master bath (left), a handsomely curved tub is placed at one end of double vanities punctuated by nearly ceiling-high niches for towels and display pieces. Instead of a medicine cabinet, the designer created a pull-out tower unit that separates his-and-hers zones. Storage units in a sleek powder room (opposite, top) mimic the curves of an elegant lacquered birch sink. A deep drawer beneath the sink holds towels; a drawer in the wall-mounted console holds bathroom necessities, out of sight beneath a trio of open display shelves. A pair of built-in hampers is concealed in a cabinet (opposite, bottom) set in what would have been lost space under a bath's pitched ceiling. Deep storage drawers tuck under the window seat.

A bathroom's lengthy tub wall (below) is enhanced by a custom storage unit designed as furniture. It suits the style of the space and also provides a huge amount of storage. A dressing table and newly upholstered stool get a prime spot at the end of a narrow bath (opposite, left). The mirrored cabinet above provides generous storage for cosmetics and medications. Bath essentials and towels are stored in the twin towers— drawers and cupboards in each—that flank the table. To differentiate individual bath functions of each section of this vanity (opposite, top right), storage cabinet height varies. Belle Epoque was the homeowners' desired style for their richly appointed bath (opposite, bottom right). The custom vanity resembles a cluster of individual pieces of fine furniture.

SPACE-STRETCHERS Squeezing additional storage space into an existing bathroom may not be easy but is rarely an impossible dream. And there are ways to do it that are not claustrophobic or traffic impediments. Best advice is purely visual: Stand in the middle of the bath and look at every stretch of available wall; also note the height of the ceiling. Your mandate here is to make every cubic inch count.

- A small corner cabinet or wall-hung shelf unit could provide a place where attractive bottles and jars could be displayed and stored. Cosmetic and bath-care product manufacturers devote much energy to packaging, so even some of the cheapest products on drugstore shelves are bottled and presented handsomely.

- If there is room to add a shallow but relatively wide shelf unit, or a bookcase in a similar scale, opt for the tallest one your bathroom can accommodate. If you keep a step stool handy, ceiling-level shelving is not inaccessible, particularly if you restrict its use to seldom-needed items. Freestanding units, from home centers and unfinished-furniture stores, come in a seemingly endless variety of sizes and shapes.

- Why strain to reach for a fresh bar of soap stashed in the back of the vanity when you could keep it, in reserve, mere inches from where you want to use it? A niche carved into one wall of a shower or a tub backsplash can hold a generous supply of bathing essentials: soaps, sponges, brushes, shampoos, conditioners. Some shower-stall niches are large enough to contain two very useful shelves.

- Having an upholstered bench in a bathroom would provide an extra layer of service to bathing hygiene. But if that bench was part of a unit containing drawers, it could supply a very welcome storage bonus.

- Creating a separate space for the toilet? Why not add a wall-hung storage unit above it—shelves or even a shallow cabinet with useful drawers?

- Here's an easy decorating trick that has a special purpose: Cover the lower portions of your bathroom walls with wainscoting. Paint it in your trim tone, then top it with a narrow shelf for displaying decorative votives, perfume bottles, and pretty containers.

MOVABLE MARVELS There's no reason you can't provide storage that will come to you rather than units that suggest that you come to them.

- A small cabinet on wheels could bring a selection of bath needs right to your elbow, its mobility justifying whatever wall space it uses when idle.

- A tray on a stand would be an attractive—and convenient— inclusion, bringing a collection of bath oils and fragrances to whoever is using the shower or tub, or even one of the sinks.

NOTABLE DETAILS Small spaces invite small solutions—modest ways to make the most of available space. Before trying to squeeze, take an inventory. Note: It's not only medications that lose potency over time; consider tossing any lotions or fragrances that haven't been touched in a year. If clutter-free, even some bath storage can be decorative, according to Dianna Holmes, a Markham, Ontario, interior designer. "If you choose an attractive container, you don't have to hide what you store; you can always put it on display. Keep mouthwash handy; contain it in a glass flask or wine decanter. To store such essentials as cotton balls, swabs, makeup brushes, and emery boards, use stainless steel canisters for sparkle as well as style."

TOWEL GEOGRAPHY Towels currently in use need to be separated from clean towels not yet in use. And, of course, there are washcloths and more than one kind of towel to deal with: bath towel, hand towel, fingertip, bath sheet, and beach or lawn towel.

- If you lack a linen closet, your towel collection can be folded and stowed on vanity shelving or in a shallow armoire either just outside the bathroom or only a few steps down the hall. Or each towel can be rolled and placed in a wine rack recruited for this quite-different purpose.

- You can display a short stack of fresh fingertip or hand towels beside each sink and bath towels on a tub ledge or a stool near the shower. Another way to display clean towels is to fold them over rungs of a short painted ladder leaned against one wall.

- Towels in daily use need drying space; they can't be scrunched or their dampness could encourage mildew. Towel bars in various lengths can be mounted—even stacked—near where the towels are needed.

- Towel rings are effective space-saving alternatives, as are hooks, either single- or multi-pronged.

QUICK SOLUTIONS

- Expand vanity capacity by attaching vinyl-covered plastic shelf units to existing fixed shelving.

- To improve cabinets' access, retrofit them with sliding shelves.

- Stack boxes covered in fabric on an open shelf to display brushes, combs, and hair accessories. Particularly in a powder room, keep sample-size soaps handy on pretty dishes in a tiered plate holder.

- Store extra towels in baskets tucked under a sink or in shelving mounted over the bathroom door.

Bookending a double vanity that has faceted glass knobs (top) are two glass-fronted cabinets that display attractive bottles and tins. Drawers and open shelves hold supplies, but drawer fronts under each undermount sink are strictly for show. Dazzling glass tiles back his-and-hers vanities (above), each with two cupboard doors. A storage tower holds bath supplies and subtly divides the space. Square porcelain vessel sinks define dual grooming areas (opposite) of a contemporary-style master bath. The chocolate-colored glass tiles contrast with the coolness of the vanity's smooth oak shelves and storage drawers.

A large storage cabinet separates the shower stall and toilet compartment (right) in a remodeled bath that uses space from former closets and two small bathrooms. Horizontally installed extra-wide beadboard covers wall areas around and behind the furniture-like double vanity with undermount sinks. Identical cast-bronze vessel sinks rest on a single sheet of half-inch-thick glass that tops a wall-wide double vanity (below, right). Directly above the diagonally shelved zone where rolled-up towels are stashed is a three-drawer unit that serves as a distinctive variation on the idea of a built-in medicine cabinet. Note that due to an infusion of liquid chemicals, the circular tiles set into the floor in front of each sink almost magically change color when stepped on. A piece of used furniture (opposite, left) was painted in two tones and plumbed by a pro, becoming a striking double vanity with square vessel sinks. Open shelves at the far end of the same bath (opposite, right) use space under a ceiling slope that was formerly wasted.

*Limestone-and-onyx vessel sinks are set
atop a custom-finished double vanity
(right and below, right) with drawers
and cupboards for bath supplies and
a wide, open shelf at the bottom for
towels. Recessed an inch into the wall,
a medicine cabinet (below) extends
outward from each mirror, providing a
shelf and shallow storage space reached
by unlatching a pair of glass-framed
doors. Because both medicine cabinet
doors swing open outward, the single-
lever faucets were installed beside rather
than behind both of the sinks.*

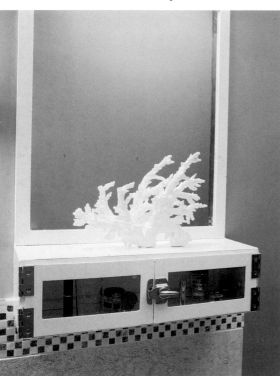

Above the twin undermount sinks in this new master bath (above) are two medicine cabinets, each with a mirrored door, set into the wall. Their shape is echoed in the shallow niche centered on the wall between them. Other niches are carved into this bath, utilizing the gaps between vertical studs: One pair, in the tub zone, places a tall space for flowers directly above a long glass-tile-lined rectangle that holds bathing products (left); a vertical niche in the shower zone (far left), also lined with glass tiles, is conveniently placed to hold a variety of soaps and shampoos.

New, but with vintage trappings, this bath was designed and built in unused attic space. A small step-up cabinet (above) adds both closed and open storage space under the slope of the ceiling. A wide ledge that extends around three sides of the room (right) is meant for bathroom items placed exactly where they are needed. Natural light pouring in through the skylights is reflected in the mirror set into the bathroom door. A basket of fresh towels (below) is placed at the base of the wide pedestal sink.

A freestanding oversize soaking tub is the centerpiece of this storage-packed master bath (above). Beyond it, in a corner configuration, is cabinetry (right) containing open shelves, glass-fronted cabinets, and closed drawers and cupboards—sufficient storage capacity to liberate limited wall space in the adjacent master bedroom. Makeup aids have a home in the shallow drawer beneath a wall cabinet (below). Inside that cabinet (below, right) are shelves that rise to the ceiling. A bath bonus is the ironing board that unfolds out of one of the drawers (below, far right).

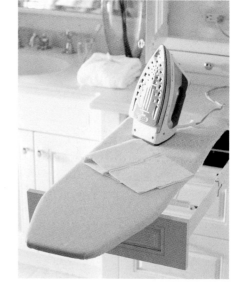

Open shelving inside a low, round-edged rolling cart (right) holds stacks of towels and an arrangement of decorative items in a bath made notable by its striking mix of materials. Wide drawers in the elongated double vanity with brushed-aluminum hardware (below) hold grooming gear and towels; medications are kept in medicine cabinets at both ends of the long wall-hung mirror unit. Steel legs stabilize the front section of the maple vanity, but the piece itself is firmly affixed to the wall. Strips of maple, installed both horizontally and vertically, create an unusual backsplash.

Open-shelf storage and a wall-plus of windows (above) create a breezy atmosphere in this upstairs bath with near woods as its privacy screen. Towels are stacked neatly on some shelves (right), and bathing needs are stored discreetly behind rippled-glass doors (far right) that slide open and shut.

Contrasting shapes and materials lend drama to a bath in a restored Boston home. The centerpiece is a Japanese-style copper soaking tub (above). Beyond it is a tall, narrow cabinet whose shelving stores towels plus bathing and grooming essentials. Across the room is an L-shaped vanity (opposite). Its marble countertop steps down six inches so that undermount and vessel sinks are on the same level.

Victorian in theme but packed with contemporary conveniences, this spectacular master bath (above) has furniture-like storage amenities designed to coordinate with furnishings used throughout the house. An elegantly ornamented arch frames the room's only mirror; directly below the center of the arch is a single undermount sink.

It is set into a notched-out section of cabinetry that, trimmed with a pair of pilasters, sllghtly expands this vanity's storage capacity. At the far end of the bath is a matching armoire, which is used to store towels and linens. A three-shelf cabinet (left), designed to hold everyday toiletries, is set into each end of the arch. All of the wood is cherry.

A surfeit of sunlight plus views of surrounding woods from a second-floor aerie (above and right) are the earmarks of this open, efficiently organized master bath. Mirrors hang from steel supports above the steel-framed, marble-topped vanity. The plumbing pipes are mostly exposed, obscured only by towels on horizontal bars. An aid to grooming, the mirrors also serve to reflect sunlight that pours into the bath through windows beyond the tub and the open-stall shower. A four-drawer chest built into the center of the vanity holds grooming essentials.

In reconfiguring but not expanding the space within this 15-by-15-foot bath, a designer placed two vanities back to back (above), separated by a nearly inch-thick wall, mirrored on both sides. Storage drawers pull out of the bow-front cabinet at the end. Three steel storage niches (above, right) are mounted in a shower-wall gap; the same arrangement exists within the shower (below). Cupboards, drawers, pull-out bins, and cabinets with frosted-glass doors supply vanity storage (right).

Cherry cabinets in this spacious master bath take their cues from Italian-style furnishings in the bedroom, creating a visual link between the two spaces. One base cabinet (above) serves as a dressing bench near the tub and also as drawer space for towels (below). Beside the double vanity (right), above which a mirror reflects the metal star on the wall above the tub, is a hutch with shelves for rolled-up towels and often-used grooming essentials. All other bath needs are partially concealed behind the hutch's ribbed-glass cabinet doors.

8 | OUT-OF-THE-WAY PLACES

JUST BECAUSE FEW PEOPLE SEE IT, you can't really deny that it's there. What? Clutter. And spaces like garages, tool and garden sheds, attics, and basements often become magnets, attracting clutter mainly because family members consider such spaces mere dumping grounds. What happens when these spaces are not used wisely is that whatever you store gets lost, overlooked, or completely forgotten. It's one thing to make storage neat, another to make it visible and accessible. As you organize storage in these far-flung locations, why not keep a log? Note by category (and date) what is stashed where, so you're not suddenly rushing from garage to tool shed to find an item you may have packed carefully and perhaps even labeled. The most painful exercise in organizing is step number one: weeding out, getting rid of what no longer works well and what is no longer needed. Be advised: Local charities welcome serviceable items. Be generous.

A vivid orange idea board adds color and creativity to a garage's back corner (opposite). Images from magazines are displayed as inspiration, along with gardening supplies and nails and screws in same-size jars, and there's plenty of open space for flowerpots, fertilizers and a giant watering can to service seed beds.

Attic space became a guest room (above), with a kid's bed atop a wide storage drawer. The ladder leads to a rooftop widow's walk. In a sleek bath (below) built over a garage, the drawer-filled vanity has its own space, made private by a barn-style sliding door.

ATTICS AND BASEMENTS

The top and bottom of a house are perfect places to store items you either use rarely or don't use at all but feel you should hang on to. Many a homeowner confesses that "ten minutes after I've given or thrown something away, I usually find I need it." So weed out attic and basement contents prudently. If something has not been used in a year or two, or a carton has been taped and tied so long that the label has faded, you should be safe in seeking a way to dispose of it.

LOFTY SOLUTIONS Homes with attics are usually top-heavy with storage overflow—all manner of material that can no longer be contained in more accessible spots. An attic's inherent messiness is often a deterrent. However, when weeded out and organized right, an attic can be a good place for items the family no longer uses regularly but cannot live without.

- Before determining which household storage should be shifted to the attic, make sure the existing structure meets the load-bearing capacity specified in your local building code. If you're uncertain, it's a good idea to talk to a builder or home inspector. Some attics are sturdy enough to store one or more grand pianos; some definitely are not.

- Raw attics are not ideal repositories for most household goods. But by adding insulation and, if necessary, ventilation, you can create a suitable comfort zone for most items, even without heating or cooling.

- Install vapor-retarding batts as insulation before laying 4-by-8-foot sheets of plywood or particleboard an inch thick across the joists.

- To protect most stored goods, lay insulation between outer wall studs and also between roof rafters. Cover with fire-rated gypsum wallboard.

MAKING ROOM AT THE TOP Before hauling anything up to the attic, prepare the space so there are no blind spots or wasted corners. Plan to arrange attic storage logically. For example, keep seasonal needs near the entrance, so you can locate and retrieve things easily.

- Build or install shelving where you find room. Note that the containers you shelve will be easier to reach than those you stack.

- For good air circulation as well as convenient access, make a point of keeping everything you store off the floor.

- Put everything in containers; loose items not only waste space but also can become damaged or lost over time.

- Transparent heavy-duty plastic containers are ideal for attic storage. They are lightweight, their lids close tightly, and their contents are always visible.

- Use a permanent marking pen to label the front, top, and sides of every container.

- Arrange items by their size and weight: large, heavy containers on lower shelves, small, light containers on upper shelving.

- Keep all of your important papers in fireproof containers or in a rented vault.

ATTIC CAVEATS Keep these dos and don'ts in mind before you haul anything up:

- DO wrap every item in bubble wrap or newspaper, as a shield against even slight fluctuations in temperature.

- DO seal containers with heavy-duty transparent tape or duct tape—for good moth, dust, and moisture protection.

- DON'T store photographs, film, packaged foods, candles, cosmetics, old phonograph records, or combustible fluids. Attic heat buildup can be damaging and often dangerous.

HOLIDAY POSTMORTEM Pack tree ornaments in sturdy wooden, plastic, or metal containers, not cardboard; arrange them by size.

- Line the bottom of each container with corrugated cardboard; glue paper cups to the liner, top ends up.

- Wrap each ornament in acid-free white tissue paper and drop into a cup; use egg cartons when storing small ornaments.

- Top with another cardboard layer and repeat. While it is okay to stack ornaments within containers, avoid putting other containers on them.

A sizable dormer adds valuable floor space to each end of what had been an unfinished attic. Here (above), a guest bedroom fills one end. The new dormer makes room for a niche on each side of the bed. One is for built-in drawers, the other for tall bookshelves, as shown.

BASEMENT ACCESS

As it's important to see everything you store, good lighting will not only make any dark basement cheerier but also expose corners and crannies that could be overlooked.

■ Overhead storage, which takes advantage of vertical space, can be hung from a basement's ceiling joists—shelving made from scraps or wood from a lumberyard.

■ Storage on wheels—rolling carts or cupboard-and-drawer units— are great for seasonal retrieval. Just roll one or more units to the foot of the stairs when you anticipate needing to access the contents.

DAMPNESS QUOTIENT Below-grade basements are inherently damp, as condensation easily penetrates concrete walls and floor.

■ Keep all basement storage off the floor. Rest storage containers or freestanding shelf units on sleepers—2-by-4's laid so there is some air space between the floor and whatever you have to store.

■ As dampness invites mildew and mold, avoid storing clothing, books, or old papers unless your basement is consistently super-dry.

■ If your basement is habitually damp, consider installing an electric dehumidifier to make sure that the space stays consistently dry.

GARAGE EFFICIENCY

CARS PLUS STORAGE Depending on the size of your garage and the number of cars it houses, plan to use both side walls plus the entire back wall for open and closed storage.

■ As with the basement, keep as much of what you store as possible off the dampness-prone concrete floor.

■ Hang such items as garden tools, axes, or even power tools on the wall with long nails or rustproof vinyl-covered hooks.

■ Hang ladders sideways, on hooks or brackets, or arrange to store them flat overhead—on ceiling rafters.

A 15-by-28-foot basement is home to a vast collection of surfboards (above), on shelves and on hooks. A hanging canvas tote (below) holds gardening gear in a well-organized garage. An efficient wall system (opposite, top) keeps tools and garden needs off the floor of a once-unused garage. Rolling cabinets and work benches complete the picture (opposite, bottom left and right). One tall cabinet on wheels is dedicated to storing summertime gear.

In a mudroom that doubles as a laundry room (below and below, right), frosted glass–door cabinets above the appliances hold laundry and cleaning supplies. Cabinets and open shelves that frame the boot-changing bench hold baskets and outdoor gear. One curtained wall of a basement bath (opposite, top) is a self-contained laundry. An all-purpose storage cabinet fills open space in the hall outside a master bedroom (opposite, bottom).

- To stow large items, use heavy-duty plastic containers or galvanized steel ones. You can stand garden tools in them or use lidded ones to protect bags of lawn seed or bird food from bugs and rodents.

- To keep hand tools and gardening implements accessible, hang them from nails or from hooks in pegboard. You can also group like items in metal or plastic buckets hung from nails or hooks.

- Place small items, such as nails, nuts, and bolts, in clear jars on eye-level shelves. Or, group like items in small, sealable plastic bags nailed to the wall. Out-of-sight items tend to be forgotten or overlooked.

SUPER-LUXE LAUNDRY ROOMS

Exposed pipes and cords, naked appliances standing forlornly on basement floors—these are true relics. Today's home laundries get sophisticated settings, with storage aplenty. A laundry room may arouse little affection, but it's one of a home's most-used places. Few laundry rooms are designed for lingering, but with rethinking they can become inviting spaces.

ON LOCATION In many homes, the washer and dryer are still in

the basement; in others, they are tucked near bedrooms or in kitchen corners. But many home designers are placing these appliances in beautifully decorated, storage-packed laundry rooms. And even the handsomest setups can be shut away with bifold doors or with pull curtains that elegantly hide this functional facility.

- Ideal laundry vignettes include either closed cabinets or open shelves, often a combination of both. And the cupboards sometimes have glass-paneled doors—clear or translucent—so that stored shapes and colors can be identified quickly.

- In the most basic laundry room arrangements, a single overhead shelf keeps detergents, softeners, and bleaches within arm's reach.

- Luxury laundry centers may include broad surfaces for handling clean clothes, ironing boards that fold out of the wall, comfortable chairs that encourage lingering and reading while the appliances spin, and perhaps even TVs and surround-sound music systems.

- Even in this era of wash-and-wear, ironing may still be an occasional essential, which is why some laundry rooms have electrically wired ironing centers mounted between wall studs so they don't project far into the room. Amenities include a plug outlet for the iron, a light, and a metal shelf to rest a hot iron on, plus a metal ironing board that's just about full size—it swivels so it can be positioned easily. And when not in use, the whole apparatus retracts into the wall and disappears.

- Stackable washers and dryers make good space-savers, no matter where you install them. Tucked behind closed doors, they will become mostly invisible components of sleek kitchen design.

- In a move toward enhancing convenience, many home laundries are being installed directly under the slope of basement stairs.

MUST-HAVES To function efficiently, even in this era of advanced technology, a home-laundry setup also needs these basic amenities:

- A laundry basket, hamper, or rolling cart that can alternately hold soiled and clean items. A two- or three-unit container would be ideal, making it possible for clothing to be separated.

- Near access to a flat surface—a table, countertop, or smooth-top appliance—on which clean clothing can be sorted and folded.

- A pole or wooden dowel to enable newly ironed or drip-dry clothes to be hung on hangers.

- If there is no ironing center, a wall rack to hold iron and ironing board.

FLOWER AND POTTING STATIONS

MAKING ARRANGEMENTS If flowers are part of your party-planning or routine decorating schemes, you need space set aside for doing floral arrangements—from home-grown or store-bought product.

- Store vases and bowls on open shelving or in closed cupboards. Whether hidden or exposed, these vessels should all be kept in one area so that they are always handy when needed and you can see them readily before deciding which size and shape you prefer.

- If your flower center has the luxury of a sink, your arranging chores are easier. If not, make sure you have a place to store a large pitcher or a hook from which to hang a bucket. Getting fresh flowers into water fast is the key to their longevity.

- Limited space should not limit your ability to create a special spot for flower arranging. A narrow freestanding base cabinet with a usable top surface could be tucked in the corner—of a laundry room or kitchen—and as long as its use remains dedicated to flower arranging, it can be no less useful than a built-in facility.

- Keep appropriate garden shears or scissors handy in drawers directly beneath your work surface. Starting a search for such arranging essentials when you have other party-planning chores to deal with wastes time.

UNDER WRAPS Anniversaries, birthdays, special occasions like the holidays—all call for gifts wrapped to suit the tone and style of the event. While it's possible to use the kitchen or dining room table for gift-wrapping, it's much better to have a place specifically reserved for such activity.

- A gift-wrap station could be anywhere a flat surface and a few shelves exist: one wall of a finished basement, a corner of a kitchen or laundry room, or even a niche in a home office.

- You should create or set aside a work surface large enough to unfurl a standard 30-inch-wide roll of wrapping paper.

- Stand rolls of gift-wrap paper in a wire-mesh basket, preferably one with wheels, so it can be rolled in and out of a closet or tall cupboard when needed.

- If you prefer to buy wrapping paper in sheets rather than rolls, you will need wide shelving so the sheets are kept flat and perennially unwrinkled.

- Thread spools of ribbon onto a long, thin wall-mounted rod. Or, press them onto paper-towel holders installed on the inside of cabinet doors. Small gift bags can also be hung on these rods, or clipped on with clothespins.

- For convenience, stow tissue paper and raffia-like filler in transparent plastic containers. Keep a coil of bubble wrap on hand to protect fragile packed items.

- Complete your wrapping station with an improvised twine or string dispenser: Invert a terra-cotta flowerpot and pull the loose end of the cord through the opening. Keep scissors handy.

- Devote one drawer to segregated gift tags, gift cards, and a collection of greeting cards to suit most occasions. Having such items in reserve and at the ready could certainly prove a needed time-saver.

- A refuse container probably should be hidden. If you have room, place it within a closed base cabinet. If not, tuck it into open space beneath a counter or table. Conceal with a curtain hung on a spring rod.

Built-in cabinets turn a forgotten corner (opposite) into an efficient flower-arranging center. A variation on this concept was built along one wall of a back hall (above): open shelves beside a wide work surface, baskets mounted in open shelves, and a waste container hidden discreetly behind a curtain.

A white-painted baker's rack (above) is loaded with baskets full of table-setting essentials on a wide, sheltered porch used for alfresco summer dining. A tote placed on a rustic bench (below, right) keeps porch clutter at bay. Mobility aids flexibility: A painted wooden carrier becomes a nest for cheery cloth napkins (below, far right). Beside the fireplace opening in this stone-faced chimney (opposite) is a slightly smaller opening, this one for log storage.

PRETTY POTTING. A potting station is a must if green-thumb chores include transferring plants from tacky plastic pots to earth-toned terra cotta. Here again, a corner or wall of a basement or garage would be a good place to create this handy amenity.

- Position a potting station near a window, if possible, to provide some sunlight and ventilation. A wall-mounted lamp or light fixture would also be beneficial. Even an adjustable lamp that can clip onto a work surface would provide an important addition to task lighting.

- Buy or build a waist-high workbench, preferably one with a shelf for flowerpots and watering cans, plus a bin for hand tools.

- Lay a cushiony rubber mat in front of the bench so you can stand for extended periods of time without straining your knees, feet, and back.

- Keep a clipboard, a calendar, and a pen or pencil within reach—on wall hooks or inside a drawer—so you can track the progress of your potting chores throughout the growing season.

DECK AND PORCH POWER

OUT-OF-SIGHT ESSENTIALS Concealment is the key to keeping outdoor entertaining sites neat and uncluttered.

- Alfresco entertaining should look effortless. Choose attractive storage units to contain needed accessories and keep them accessible.

- Small-scale rustic pieces—either from thrift shops or tag sales—would work well in a sheltered outdoor setting. Make sure what you acquire has good storage potential as well as decorating interest.

- Built-in outdoor cooking appliances should be installed in a setting that includes cupboards where supplies can be stashed. Hooks to hold cooking utensils are also important.

ORGANIZING TOOL AND GARDEN SHEDS

CLUTTER CAVEATS An outdoor shed may start out as a place to store fertilizer, tools, and lawn seed. But often it becomes a receptacle for items that have no place being there—crowding the items that do belong, thus making them virtually inaccessible.

- Optimize space. Even if the shed you buy or build already has shelving, you can probably add more. If there are vertical studs, you can use 1-by-3 scrap lumber to fashion shelves between them.

- To improvise dual-purpose storage, install shallow shelves between studs; front each section of stud shelving with pegboard mounted on piano hinges. Hang small tools on pegboard hooks and store seed packets in small boxes on the shelving inside.

- Or, consider hanging shelves for seed packets on the inside of the shed door. And why not suspend those most-used small tools from rows of hooks installed there?

- A bucket, which you can hang by its handle or set on a shelf, can be a good, compact catchall for loose items and small tools.

- Hang long-handled tools on shed walls with hooks or nails. Or, use one or more spaces between studs for tool storage; to keep loose tools from falling out, try attaching a strip of 1-by-2-inch strapping lumber to a pair of studs at both knee and waist height.

- Another possibility: Cut off the tops and bottoms of any size tin cans, and cut away jagged edges. Nail cans vertically to studs or shed walls at waist height to create places in which to stand inverted tall tools.

- Hang bamboo stakes and grow-through frames on overhead hooks.

- Childproof the shed by storing weed killers and insecticides out of easy reach—on a high shelf or in lockable storage. It may also make sense to put a padlock on the shed door.

- Keep whatever you store off the floor. Whether your shed floor is wood, steel, concrete, or raw earth, it is unlikely to resist dampness.

- Store sacks of fertilizer, peat moss, and mulch in large containers or on skids to keep them off the floor or the ground. Or, improvise skids by laying chunks of scrap lumber on bricks or blocks made of 2-by-4's.

- Flowerpots take storage space, so stack them by size. Remember, however, that terra-cotta pots may not stack well. Separating them with rag scraps will make them easier to pull apart when needed.

The compact design of a self-contained garden shed (this page) has shelves and hooks—there are no wasted spaces. Hooks on the inside of doors create important bonus storage spaces. Step-saving storage guided designers of two outdoor kitchens (opposite). Each has closed spaces to store the essentials of outdoor cooking and entertaining. Cooking tools hang on the side of one unit (opposite, top); an all-weather sink with storage underneath completes the wall-wide Southwest design (opposite, bottom).

RESOURCES

Local hardware, office-supply, and big-box stores display shelving, shelf and drawer dividers, and sometimes cabinetry. If you don't find what you are looking for locally, check out the following sources, each with national reach. Even if you do see what you like, feel free to comparison-shop online before purchasing.

ACE HARDWARE

866-290-5334
www.acehardware.com
Basement, bath, closet, garage, and kitchen organizing systems; storage carts, drawers, shelving, totes

ARISTOKRAFT, INC.

812-482-2527
www.aristokraft.com
Kitchen base cabinets with inside-door shelving; roll-out/pull-out shelf units, roll-out pantries, corner cabinets with rotating shelves, drawer/door spice racks, cutlery trays. Bathroom vanity door racks, pull-out shelving

BROOKSTONE

800-846-3000
www.brookstone.com
Modular kitchen shelving systems. Bedroom open-shelf nightstand, adjustable reading table. Wall-hung bathroom towel storage

THE COMPANY STORE

888-266-8246
www.thecompanystore.com
Storage ottomans/benches, under-bed storage, console with closed cupboard, nesting baskets, wall shelf with hooks, end/side tables with shelves/drawers, corner bench and shelf, bench unit with hooks/shelf, bookcase-cupboard unit

THE CONTAINER STORE

800-786-7315
www.containerstore.com
Kitchen drawer organizers, rolling storage, baker's rack. Closet systems. Home-office file carts, stackable storage. Bathroom organizer trays

CRATE & BARREL

800-967-6696
www.crate&barrel.com
Kitchen storage bowls, canister, jars, trays, utensil holder, dish/spice racks, wine storage, hanging pot racks, silverware storage

FRONTGATE

888-263-9850
www.frontgate.com
Closet storage drawers/shelves, trouser/shoe racks. Bedroom charging stations, fold-out makeup trunk, floor mirror with storage

GARAGETEK

866-664-2724
www.garagetek.com
Garage cabinets, shelving, ceiling systems, work/hobby stations, storage bins/brackets

GET ORGANIZED

800-803-9400
www.shopgetorganized.com
Media cabinet with drawers, under-shelf wrap rack, CD/DVD/video cassette drawers, revolving book storage, bench with baskets. Closet shelf dividers, shoe/garment/earring racks. Kitchen can storage, cabinet plate/pot-lid organizers, under-sink shelving, under-shelf organizers, recycling bins, slide-out pantry, wine rack. Laundry room clothes caddy, drying rack. Bedroom under-bed shoe organizers. Golf/fishing rod organizer racks

GLADIATOR GARAGEWORKS

By Whirlpool Corporation
866-342-4089
www.gladiatorgw.com
Workbenches with storage, wall system and components, steel storage cabinets

GRANDIN ROAD

888-668-5962
www.grandinroad.com
Media consoles, entertainment centers, storage ottomans, bookcases, mudroom lockers. Kitchen wine hutches. Home-office storage systems, desks

THE HOME DEPOT

800-430-3376
www.homedepot.com
Shelving/shelving systems; storage totes/baskets/hooks/racks. Laundry room hampers/baskets. Bathroom medicine cabinets/vanities/towel bars/hooks. Deck/tool/garden-gear storage. Garage shelving/cabinets/workbenches, ceiling/wall-mounted storage. Attic/kitchen/pantry/laundry room/office storage

HOME TRENDS

800-815-0814
www.shophometrends.com
Bedroom under-bed shoe organizer. Closet shelf dividers, plastic garment/blanket bags, jewelry storage, over-door hooks. Kitchen bakeware/lid racks, place-mat holder, sliding insert drawers, under-shelf baskets, spice storage. Laundry room drying rack, utility cart

IKEA

800-833-6687
www.ikea.com
Freestanding storage units/accessories for living/dining rooms, kitchen, bedroom, closet, bathroom

KRAFTMAID

888-562-7744
www.kraftmaid.com
General kitchen/laundry room/bathroom/home office storage. Specialized storage—entertainment centers, linen cabinet, wine rack, foyer ensembles, foot-of-bed chests, nightstands, roll-out CD/DVD trays

LEE VALLEY TOOLS

800-267-8034
www.leevalley.com
Kitchen wall-mount storage system. Family room multi-media pull-out storage, shelf dividers, CD racks/drawers

LEVENGER

800-667-8034
www.levenger.com
Office desk drawer/file drawer divider; book boxes, lap desks, revolving bookcase, desktop organizers/accessories

LILLIAN VERNON

800-901-9291
www.lillianvernon.com
Kitchen rolling storage/laundry/recycling carts, spice/wine racks, canisters, over-door pantry organizer, dish rack/caddy, plastic-bag dispenser, storage bowls/bottles/holders/shakers, paper towel/napkin holders, tiered wire baskets, breadbox, compost keeper. Closet/drawer organizers, sweater/shoe boxes, valet tray, CD caddy

LOWE'S

800-445-6937
www.lowes.com
Bathroom medicine/over-toilet cabinets, vanities, robe/over-door hooks. Closet organizers, freestanding cabinets/shelf units. Kitchen drawer organizers, wire basket sets, slide-out basket storage, pot racks, pegboard hooks. Garage tool chests, cabinets, wheeled storage, ceiling/wall storage, heavy-duty wall hooks, bike stand/hook, ladder hook, wheeled storage box, garden tool organizer. Outdoor metal/vinyl/wood sheds and accessories

OFFICE MAX

800-283-7674
www.officemax.com
Bookcases, shelving, computer carts/stands. Office desks, desk organizers/accessories, file cabinets/accessories

ORGANIZE EVERYTHING

800-600-9817
www.organize-everything.com
Kitchen cabinet/shelf organizers, rolling carts, utility caddies/buckets/holders, drawer/cutlery organizers, plastic-bag dispensers, coupon organizers, baskets, bins, boxes, napkin/paper towel holders. Laundry baskets/drying racks, utility carts, wall grid system, hampers/sorters. Closet system/components/accessories. Storage cubes, under-bed storage. Bathroom cabinets, cosmetics organizers, drawer trays, hooks/racks, shelving, étagères, towel bars/racks, toilet-paper storage. Craft/hobby organizers. Overhead garage/attic storage, tool racks/accessories, key storage

ORGANIZE-IT

800-210-7712
www.organize-it.com
Decorative/utility shelving. Closet systems/accessories. Garage organizers. Kitchen drawer organizers, storage accessories. Laundry room over-door valets, standing hanger holder. Bathroom over-cabinet towel bar, shower caddy. Office letter holder/key rack, drawer/vertical file organizers

PIER 1 IMPORTS

800-245-4595
www.pier1.com
Decorative baskets, boxes,
hampers

POLIFORM USA

800-421-1220
www.poliformusa.com
Contemporary-style bookcases,
sideboards, wardrobes, walk-in
closet systems

POTTERY BARN

888-779-5176
www.potterybarn.com
Foyer/bedroom/kitchen/laundry
room/media room/home-office
furniture/accessories. Wall-
hung ledges/shelves. Storage
tables/cubes/benches, coat
racks/hooks. Jewelry/valet boxes;
recharging station. Baskets, metal
key cabinet, bookcases, wine/
glassware storage

REV-A-SHELF

800-667-8721
www.revashelf.net
Kitchen/bath cabinets/storage
accessories. Pantry fittings/
complete systems. Patio storage
racks/carts

RUBBERMAID HOME PRODUCTS

888-895-2110
www.rubbermaid.com
Buckets, bins, cabinet/drawer
organizers, deck storage boxes,
food containers, garage shelving,
hampers, holiday storage, laundry
baskets, shower organizers,
outdoor buildings/sheds

SAUDER WOODWORKING

800-523-3987
www.sauder.com
Bedroom armoires, chests,
dressers, nightstands, modular
storage. Family room CD/DVD
storage, entertainment centers/
armoires, TV carts. Office file
cabinets, computer armoires/
carts/desks. Utility carts/stands,
shelf units, bookcases, wardrobes
Craft storage systems/furniture

SCHULTE DISTINCTIVE STORAGE

800-669-3225
www.schultestorage.com
Clothes/linen closet systems.
Freestanding stationary/wheeled
storage drawers. Home office setups. Pantry/laundry room storage.
Garage systems, wall storage—
lawn and garden, sports gear

STACKS AND STACKS

800-761-5222
www.stackssandstacks.com
Bedroom chest, armoires,
dressers, nightstands, storage
beds; kids' desks, dressers,
nightstands, bookshelves. Hall
storage bench, coat racks.
Entertainment centers/armoires,
TV stands, multi-media storage.
Family/living room decorative
chests/étagères, storage cubes/
ottomans. Office desks, file/
storage cabinets, computer carts/
armoires/work station

STAPLES

800-378-27553
www.staples.com
Desks, desktop storage
accessories, bookcases, file
cabinets, armoires, storage
carts/stands

THE STORAGE STORE

800-600-9817
www.thestoragestore.com
Kitchen counter/tabletop/drawer
organizers, pot racks, carts, spice
racks. Closet clothing/shoe/
accessories storage; drawer/
jewelry organizers, garment
racks/bags. Bathroom cosmetics
organizer, towel racks/hooks,
shower caddies. Laundry room
clothes racks/carts, ironing board
storage. Multi-purpose shelving,
chests, wall units, media storage,
bookcases, storage cubes/boxes/
drawer units, lidded ottoman.
Office furniture, accessories.
Garage wall/grid systems, boxes,
bins, tool storage

TAYLOR GIFTS

800-829-1133
www.taylorgifts.com
Stackable storage, storage
beds/benches, hanging makeup
organizer, document files/boxes,
mobile pantry, computer desk
components, under-bed shoe
organizer, laundry room storage

WEST ELM

888-922-4119
www.westelm.com
Bedroom dressers, nightstands,
wall shelving, closet organizers,
storage headboards/ottomans/
cubes. Living/dining room
consoles, sideboards, wine bar,
bookcases, shelf units, coffee
table with shelves. Home office
desks, file cabinets, bookcases,
media storage. Bathroom console,
ladder rack, shelving, modular
storage, towel bars/rings/hooks

CLOSET ORGANIZERS

The following are closet-system design firms whose consultations are usually free. Fees for actual closet designs or redesigns, though billed up front, are ultimately applied to any custom design you commission. Note that many such firms—local as well as national—have expanded services, thus providing products, accessories, and design solutions to satisfy virtually every storage need in the house.

CALIFORNIA CLOSETS

888-336-9707
www.californiaclosets.com

CLOSET FACTORY

800-634-9000
www.closetfactory.com

CLOSETMAID

800-874-0008
www.closetmaid.com

CLOSET ORGANIZER SOURCE

866-783-2852
www.closetorganizersource.com

CLOSETS BY DESIGN

888-500-9215
www.closetsbydesign.com

CLOSETS TO GO

888-312-7424
www.closetstogo.com

EASYCLOSETS.COM

800-910-0129
www.easyclosets.com

ACKNOWLEDGMENTS & PHOTO CREDITS

The author wishes to dedicate this book to the memory of Olivia L. Monjo, a visionary editor-in-chief who led and inspired her magazine staff through times of triumph as well as despair; to colleague Leslie Plummer Clagett, an editor whose *Kitchens & Baths* magazine originally contained some of the most informative materials in *Store It!*; and to Dorothée Walliser at Filipacchi Publishing, whose creative impulses and strong editorial drive have produced an extraordinary catalog of books.

Front cover: (top, left) Eric Roth, (top, right) James Yochum; (middle) David Duncan Livingston, (bottom, left) John Gould Bessler, (bottom, right) Gridley + Graves. Back cover: (top, left) Keith Scott Morton, (top, center) Tria Giovan/ JS Creations, Inc., (top, right) Aaron Cameron Muntz, (middle) Robert Reck, (bottom, left) Philip Clayton Thompson, (bottom, right) Evan Joseph.

Page 1: Erik Johnson; 2: John Gruen; 3: Michael Partenio; 6: Gridley + Graves; 7 (top): John Gould Bessler; 7 (bottom): Timothy Bell; 8: Eric Roth; 10 (top): Eric Roth; 10 (bottom): Michael Weschler; 11 (left): Chris Vaccaro; 11 (right): Hulya Kolabas; 12: Erik Johnson; 13 (all): John Gould Bessler; 14: Aimee Herring; 15 (left): Eric Roth; 15 (right): Keith Scott Morton; 16: Eric Roth; 17: John Gould Bessler; 18: Deborah Ory; 20: Gridley + Graves; 21: John Gruen; 22: Keith Scott Morton; 23: Susan McWhinney; 24: Deborah Ory; 25: Claudio Santini; 26: John Gruen; 27: Aimee Herring; 28: Chris Vaccaro; 29 (left): Erik Johnson; 29 (top and bottom, right): Keith Scott Morton; 30: Len Lagrua; 31: Philip Clayton Thompson; 32: Matthew Millman; 33 (left): Erik Johnson; 33 (top and bottom, right): Aaron Cameron Muntz; 34: Gridley + Graves; 36: J. Savage Gibson; 37: David Duncan Livingston; 38: Gridley + Graves; 39: Alexandra Rowley; 40-41 (all): Gridley + Graves; 42 (top): Mark Lohman; 42 (bottom): James Yochum; 43 (top, left):

Gridley + Graves; 43 (top, right): Emily Minton Redfield; 43 (bottom, right): Robin Stubbert; 44 (left): Evan Joseph; 44 (right): David Duncan Livingston; 45 (left): David Duncan Livingston; 45 (right): Alex Hayden; 46-47 (all): Ed Gohlich; 48: Tim Fuller; 49: Robert Reck; 50 (all): David Duncan Livingston; 51 (top): Alex Hayden; 51 (bottom): Robert Reck; 52 (left): Gridley + Graves; 52 (right): Deborah Ory; 53 (left): James Yochum; 53 (top, right): J. Savage Gibson; 53 (center and bottom, right): Gridley + Graves; 54 (left): John Gould Bessler; 54 (right): J. Savage Gibson; 55 (left): Evan Joseph; 55 (top, right): Robin Stubbert; 55 (bottom, right): Ken Gutmaker; 56 (top and center, left, and top, right): John Gould Bessler; 56 (bottom): Joseph DeLeo; 57 (all): Jeff McNamara; 58 (top, left/center/right): Matthew Millman, Gridley + Graves, all rights reserved; 58 (middle, left/center/ right): Matthew Millman, David Duncan Livingston, Ken Gutmaker; 58 (bottom, left/center/right): Lydia Gould Bessler, Robert Reck, Lydia Gould Bessler; 59 (top, left/center/right): Alexandra Rowley, Ken Gutmaker, Kate Roth; 59 (middle, left/center/right): Michael Weschler, Evan Joseph, Lydia Gould Bessler; 59 (bottom, left/right): Alexandra Rowley, Gridley + Graves; 60: Keith Scott Morton; 62: Alex Hayden; 63: Evan Joseph; 64: Claudio Santini; 65 (left): Jeff McNmara; 65 (right): Matthew Millman; 66 (top): Tria Giovan; 66 (bottom): John Gould Bessler; 67 (top): James Yochum; 67 (bottom): Matthew Millman; 68 (left): Jeff McNamara; 68 (right): Casey Dunn; 69 Erik Rank; 70 (both): Eric Piasecki; 71: James Yochum: 72 (top): James Yochum; 72 (bottom): Gridley + Graves; 73: Mark Samu; 74 (left and top, right): David Duncan Livingston; 74 (bottom, right): Jeff McNamara; 75 (left): James Yochum; 75 (right): Sam Gray; 76: Matthew Millman; 77 (all): Robin Stubbert; 78-79: Scott Pease; 80 (left): Michael Parenio; 80 (right): Mark Lohman; 81 (left): Alexandra Rowley; 81 (right):

John Gruen; 82 (left): Alex Hayden; 82 (right): Paul Whicheloe; 83: James Yochum; 84 (both): David Duncan Livingston; 85 (left): Ken Gutmaker; 85 (right): Gridley + Graves; 86: Tria Giovan; 87: John Gould Bessler; 88: Jamie Hadley; 90 (top): Joe Schmelzer; 90 (bottom): John Ellis; 91: Philip Clayton-Thompson; 92: Kate Roth; 93: Angus McRitchie; 94 (top): Kate Roth; 94 (bottom): Aaron Cameron Muntz; 95 (both): Jamie Hadley; 96: Sam Gray; 97: Beth Singer; 98 (top): Evan Joseph; 98 (center and bottom): Len Lagrua; 99: Evan Joseph; 100: Mark Lund; 101: Emily Minton Redfield; 102-103: Janet Mesic-Mackie; 104: David Duncan Livingston; 107 (top): James Hadley; 106 (bottom): Gridley + Graves; 107 (top): Grey Crawford; 107 (bottom): Ed Gohlich; 108: Melabee M. Miller; 109 (top, left): Joe Schmelzer; 109 (top, right): John Gould Bessler; 109 (bottom): Jeff McNamara; 110 (top): Emily Jenkins Followill; 110 (bottom): John Gould Bessler; 111: James Yochum; 112 (top): Paula Illingworth; 112 (bottom): John Gould Bessler; 113 (all): Timothy Bell; 114 (all): Kate Roth; 115 (all): Ken Gutmaker; 116 (all): Philip Clayton-Thompson; 117 (all): John Gould Bessler; 118 (both) Tria Giovan/JS Creations, Inc.; 119 (all): Ken Gutmaker; 120: Sam Gray; 121 (top, left): Sam Gray; 120 (bottom and right): Gridley + Graves; 122 (both) Casey Dunn; 124 (all): Werner Segarra; 125 (all): Mark Samu; 126: Evan Joseph; 128 (top): Chris Vaccaro; 128 (bottom): Erik Johnson; 129: Erik Johnson; 130 (top): Claudio Santini; 130 (bottom): Evan Joseph; 131 (all): Evan Joseph; 132 (both): John Gould Bessler; 133 (top): Eric Striffler; 133 (bottom): David Duncan Livingston; 134: Tim Fuller; 135: John Gould Bessler; 136 (all): Michael Partenio; 137: Tria Giovan; 138 (both): Gridley + Graves; 139 (all): Hulya Kolabas.